A Middle Mosaic

P9-AZU-428

NCTE Editorial Board: Jacqueline Bryant, Kermit Campbell, Xin Liu Gale, Sarah Hudelson, Gerald R. Oglan, Helen Poole, Jackie Swensson, Gail Wood, Faith Z. Schullstrom, Chair, ex officio, Peter Feely, ex officio

A Middle Mosaic

A Celebration of Reading, Writing, and Reflective Practice at the Middle Level

Edited by

Elizabeth Close
University at Albany, State University of New York

Katherine D. Ramsey
River Oaks Baptist School, Houston, Texas

National Council of Teachers of English
1111 W. Kenyon Road, Urbana, Illinois 61801-1096

Staff Editor: Rita D. Disroe

Interior Design: Doug Burnett

Cover Design: Jenny Jensen Greenleaf

NCTE Stock Number: 00341-3050

©2000 by the National Council of Teachers of English.

All rights reserved. No part of this publication may be reproduced or transmitted in any form or by any means, electronic or mechanical, including photocopy, or any information storage and retrieval system, without permission from the publisher. Printed in the United States of America.

It is the policy of NCTE in its journals and other publications to provide a forum for the open discussion of ideas concerning the content and the teaching of English and the language arts. Publicity accorded to any particular point of view does not imply endorsement by the Executive Committee, the Board of Directors, or the membership at large, except in announcements of policy, where such endorsement is clearly specified.

Library of Congress Cataloging-in-Publication Data

A middle mosaic: a celebration of reading, writing, and reflective practice at the middle level/edited by Elizabeth Close, Katherine D. Ramsey.
    p. cm.
   Includes bibliographical references.
   "NCTE stock number: 00341-3050"—T.p. verso.
   ISBN 0-8141-0034-1
    1. Language arts (Secondary)—United States—Congresses. 2. English language—Study and teaching (Secondary)—United States—Congresses. 3. English language—United States—Composition and exercises—Congresses. 4. Reflection (Philosophy)—Congresses. I. Title: Celebration of reading, writing, and reflective practice at the middle level. II. Close, Elizabeth, 1941– III. Ramsey, Katherine D., 1944–

LB1631.A2 2000
428'.0071'2—dc21

                                        00-042378

Contents

Introduction   vii

I. Literature and Literacy at the Middle Level   **1**

1. When Reading Is Stupid: The Why, How, and What to
   Do about It   3
   Jeffrey D. Wilhelm

2. From Hall Talk to Classroom Talk to Book Talk: Helping
   Struggling Readers Connect to Reading   11
   Kylene Beers

3. Teaching Literature through Thematic Units   21
   Mary Santerre

4. Nonfiction and Young Readers   25
   Robert C. Small Jr.

5. Literature and Lessons of the Holocaust: Theory
   and Practice   32
   Marlene B. Hartstein and Karen Zelde Schejtman Sultan

6. Telling Lewis Hine's Story: Russell Freedman's
   Kids at Work   40
   Myra Zarnowski

7. Footprints in the Mud: Reading Science   52
   Petey Young

II. Reflective Practice in the Middle   **59**

8. Sweating the Small Stuff: When Spelling Is More Than
   Small Stuff   61
   Rebecca Bowers Sipe

9. Literacy Narratives   67
   Cathy Fleischer
   Literacy Narratives: Knowing Students   73
   Jennifer Hannick Walsh
   Literacy Narratives: Working with Parents   77
   Julie A. King

10. The Writer's Notebook: A Place to Think   80
    Janet Angelillo and Anna Danon Reduce

III. The Nature and Needs of Students at the Middle Level   85

11. The Middle Schooler   87
    Jim Johnston

12. A Habit of the Heart: Service Learning   91
    Martha M. Magner

13. Interdisciplinary Teaming in the Middle School   95
    Lois T. Stover

14. Advisory: Building Relationships   100
    Martha M. Magner

15. Middle Level Teacher Preparation   104
    Judith A. Hayn

16. Vertical Connections   113
    Lanny van Allen

Appendix 1: The Middle School Mosaic: A Brief History   119

Appendix 2: A Middle School Mosaic: What a Difference a Day Makes 122

Editors   129

Introduction

Shortly after the first Middle School Mosaic in Detroit in 1997, Carolyn Lott, chair of the Secondary Section Steering Committee, suggested that we publish a collection of proceedings to celebrate its success. We were unsure of exactly what kind of response we might get or how many people would be able to gather their notes into a publishable form. Therefore, we sent out a call for manuscripts and waited nervously. We should never have worried. Middle level educators are always creative, eager to be involved, and responsive to the needs of their colleagues. The responses we received reflect both the enthusiasm and varied interests of the presenters at this Mosaic and of educators at this level.

We do not intend here to present an all-encompassing collection of essays for middle level educators. The very design of this book determined what we could include: snapshots of what presenters had to say on one day at one convention. This plan put limitations on our contributors, who worked hard to capture their presentations in writing. At the same time, we are impressed with the effort our writers made to cite sources and ground their presentations in research. This book should provide readers with some of the flavor of the first Mosaic and the excitement felt by its participants. The resulting collection, as much of a mosaic as any middle level language arts classroom, reflects the diversity we find at the middle, and is an overview of the complicated nature of middle level English education. It is not a complete view, nor was it ever intended to be so. It is, however, a good starting place.

As the manuscripts arrived, it became very clear that we had three distinct categories. This natural division made our work easy. Reaching the needs of a wide variety of backgrounds, skill levels, and interests presents enormous challenges and raises many concerns for middle level educators. Often teachers complain that students cannot read, yet they do not feel they can teach reading or that they are responsible for it. Others grapple with the issues of what literacy is and how they can address literacy with middle-grade students. The first section of this book examines some of these concerns by looking at ways to improve reading, broaden the definition of literacy and literature, and address important issues through choices of literature.

Addressing literacy also means encouraging reflective teaching and learning. Outstanding practice is a result of continuing and deliberate learning on the part of the teacher. The essays in the second section focus on ways in which teachers can learn more about themselves, their students, and the ways to support students so that students can learn more about themselves.

The final section of this book contains the essays that look at the nature and needs of middle level students and educators. To even begin to understand the demands of teaching at this level requires strong knowledge of these issues. The middle grades represent a transition in many areas. Students are developing and changing quickly, and they struggle with who they are and where they want to go. Teachers are intimately involved in the day-to-day growth of their students. They understand that teachers and students are learning together and that they are often students and facilitators themselves. The writers in this section give the reader a taste for middle level concerns with the hope that the reader will look for further information in the resources suggested.

Realizing that this book was intended to present a limited taste of middle level education, we could see that having suggestions for additional reading would guide readers to other sources and ideas. In some cases the writers provided citations and/or suggested reading lists. Where reading lists were not provided or where we felt more titles would be useful, we added some suggestions of our own.

Our call for manuscripts was sent only to the participants of a single conference; therefore, many topics are not included in this work. For example, exchanges about cooperative learning or multiple intelligences, two important topics for middle level educators, are not addressed here. We do not have essays about scaffolding literature discussions, about developing a reading/writing workshop, or about ways to address a variety of multicultural issues through literature. This collection is part of the growing voice of middle level education at the National Council of Teachers of English. Ideally, it will serve as a stimulus for other middle level educators to contribute their voices either by writing for publication or by sharing their expertise at conferences and conventions. We hope this collection will provide educators new to the middle level with tools to initiate their journeys. Those with more experience should find new understandings and directions to consider.

We owe a special thank you to Martha Magner. As program chair for the Junior High School/Middle School Assembly (JHS/MS) in 1997, she first chose the title "Middle School Mosaic" to describe their session in Detroit. We have used part of that title for the entire program each year and have chosen to use part of it as the title for this book.

I Literature and Literacy at the Middle Level

How can I make reading relevant to my students' lives?

How do I engage all students in literacy activities?

How can I help my students develop critical thinking skills?

How can I use my students' interest to support their learning?

What literary works should I include in my curriculum?

How should I organize my curriculum?

How do I achieve a balance among literary genres?

How can I make my literature instruction meaningful to other disciplines?

Middle level teachers ask these and many other questions about the teaching of literacy and literature on a daily basis, and many of the workshops at the first Middle School Mosaic attempted to address these concerns. Each of the writers in this section takes a careful look at one or more of these important questions. The answers proposed by these presenters should give classroom teachers starting points for developing their own responses.

Jeffrey Wilhelm focuses on the ways that boys respond to reading assignments and how their behavior suggests ways that might more fully engage male readers in literature activities. He explains how he connects current events and current interests to classroom activities and describes some of the activities he uses.

Kylene Beers uses her research with struggling readers to support her view that all readers need literature selections that are relevant to their lives. She discusses using thematic units as a way of reaching reluctant readers and suggests strategies to support struggling readers. She offers many sources of information and ways of engaging students in discussion.

Mary Santerre shares her experiences using thematic units within a traditional curriculum. She lists the steps she uses in planning for such units and explains how the units fit within the course requirements.

Robert Small, arguing that nonfiction should be treated as a literary form, discusses the importance of nonfiction for the middle school reader and offers reasons why we need to include more nonfiction in the curriculum. He also provides information about three outstanding sources of information about nonfiction material.

Continuing the discussion of nonfiction, Marlene Hartstein and Karen Sultan offer techniques for teaching about the Holocaust. They include a list of ideas and resources that provide a substantial base for teachers interested in beginning a study of this topic.

Myra Zarnowski also feels that nonfiction is an important element of the English classroom. Her discussion of *Kids at Work* by Russell Freedman offers ways of helping students understand the lives of people from the past. She also provides teaching suggestions that give teachers ways to apply her theories both to this particular work and to other pieces as well.

Finally, Petey Young presents an argument for treating science reading as literature and encourages daily oral reading of science materials to build an ear for the rhythm of science. She also offers practical teaching suggestions that are immediately applicable and that can encourage interdisciplinary teaching.

These essays will not provide all the answers about reading and literacy for the middle level teacher; they do, however, suggest new directions, varied techniques, and different materials. Newer teachers will find starting points for building their curriculum, more experienced teachers should discover ideas that will stimulate thinking about curriculum, and administrators should find ideas for further investigation.

1 When Reading Is Stupid: The Why, How, and What to Do about It

Jeffrey D. Wilhelm
University of Maine, Orono, Maine

One who learns from one who is learning drinks from a running stream.
> —Native American saying

Knowledge is not something you have; knowledge is something you do.
> —Barbara Libby

Reading don't fix no Chevies.
> —Jimmy Bocca

"Let's face it, Mr. Wilhelm," a student named Josh once told me, "you can have a pretty cool life without ever reading anything."

I think I understand where Josh is coming from, and I also think that though he might live a "cool" life without reading, it would certainly be an impoverished one. I've dedicated my life's work, like many teachers, to the notion that literacy is a foundational educational competency and a profoundly powerful way of knowing about the self and the world and of moving from knowledge to taking meaningful action in the world.

Josh doesn't share my view, and so he resists reading. To overcome his resistance and assist him to read powerfully, I need first for him to see reading as a personally relevant and socially significant pursuit. To help Josh and the many other students I teach who share his attitude, I've begun interviewing students from middle and high school, as well as various groups of adults, about their reading experiences and what makes these experiences meaningful or frustrating. After nearly five hundred interviews, many different themes have emerged. Here, I would like to explore just a few that are particularly salient for males, both schoolboys and adults, who resist reading and who in general indicate that they find reading "stupid."

Why Reading Is Stupid

The most salient themes to emerge from my interviews with reluctant male readers revolve around relevance, competence, and agency.

First, these readers simply do not see how reading is relevant to their "real life," how it speaks to their concerns, or how it might be useful to them, personally, as they pursue their concerns and make their way in the world. Second, they indicate in various ways that they are not really that good at reading, express frustration that they don't really know "how to do it," and add that there are lots of other things that they are good at doing and would rather do. Finally, this group indicates, as in the quote above from Jimmy Bocca, that reading neither brings about nor leads to any kind of real work or accomplishment. They often argue and demonstrate in various ways that they wish to actively exert themselves on the world. They conceive of reading as too passive, too sedentary, and too much "about mushy, girly stuff," as one seventh grader put it, to be of "any use whatsoever." Boys obviously crave connection to the world as much as girls do; however, they tend to express their connection and emotions through action (Pollack, 1998). Boys relate to others and define themselves by "doing stuff" (cf. Pollack), and they believe that reading is "not a way of doing or making anything," as Josh put it to me.

What Can WE Do about It?

I contend that my most reluctant and resistant readers aren't really resisting reading as such. Rather, they are resisting the technology of school—and the way reading is taught and pursued in the context of school. I propose that as teachers we can help students overcome the notion that "reading is stupid" by foregrounding and addressing three important concerns often ignored in schools. By doing so, we can help our students take on a productive attitude toward reading; assist them to recognize, learn, and exercise more powerful reading strategies; and help them create knowledge through their reading that can be used in meaningful, personal, and highly social ways.

These three issues are the Why, the How, and the What of reading. I mean by this that we must concern ourselves first with communicating the importance and use of reading by motivating readers and framing what will be read in personally interesting and powerful ways (Why). Usually in school, we read literature as an artifact instead of as an argument or as a call to social action. We must also pay attention to the procedures and "how to" of reading, and we must help students transform and use their reading to do real work (How). Finally, we should not only organize curricula around real problems of concern to kids but also read any texts that help us see the multiple cultural perspectives around an issue and that help us address these issues (What). This perspective means that we will necessarily reconceive the notion of "text" in school as we read more nonfiction, go to electronic sources, and begin to think of artifacts and people as "texts" to be read in order to help us understand the world and take action in it. In this context, we will still read literature; however, we will read it in much more purposeful ways, in ways that will help us forge connections to others and to higher human purposes.

"Why Should I Do This Stuff?": Motivation and Framing

According to a favorite quotation of mine from Neil Postman (1995), "for the student with an adequate why, almost any how or what will do."

The adults in my study told me that they found reading meaningful when they read to learn how to do something, to inform decision making, or to prepare for taking some kind of action. Those who enjoyed literature found it a way of exploring ways of relating to others and of being in the world. They also found that literature informed how they "did" and "decided" things.

I propose that these very purposes should be made the purposes of school reading. Instead of covering content such as the history of American literature, or reading particular authors, such as Fitzgerald and Hemingway, I think the curriculum should be organized around "contact zones" (cf. Bizzell, 1994; Pratt, 1991). Contact zones are important issues that are of great significance and that are truly under dispute, and around which there are a variety of different cultural perspectives. Though my work with students did not always include the cultural notions in as full a way as I would have liked, we always considered "facts" as social constructions and tried to achieve dialogue with positions different from our own before making decisions that would inform our social behavior.

As I look in today's newspapers I see several such contact zones at play. For instance, should public officials be held accountable for private acts? This question remains a hotly contended cultural issue, and one about which we must make a personal, if not a social, decision. I see in a particular article that the French public cannot understand what "you Americans are on about! You still think you are Puritans!"

Another front-page issue regards the fishing industry here in Maine. Should we restrict the number of lobsters harvested to ensure the future vitality of the lobster population? There are various perspectives on the matter, all invoking studies that support their points of view. Who is right? Where should I come down on these issues, and how should I act once I have decided? A third front-page issue concerns whether we need a law to protect the rights and the safety of a minority population. After two referenda on this issue, our state is still deeply divided, the debate continues, and several local communities have taken the issue into their own hands by passing town ordinances.

In my own teaching, I try to organize reading around issues of interest to my students. Reading suddenly becomes highly purposeful as students read to understand various positions within the zone, to stake out and argue for their own position, and to decide how they should act and behave based on their position.

One of my middle school language arts classes decided to explore the contact zone of sports: does participation in sports make you a better person? We read autobiographies and sports psychology, explored issues of gender and sport, interviewed a professor from the university, surfed the Internet and raised the issue in chatrooms. We ended up drafting a proposal for required intramural sports, though several students in the class chose to express a dissident view.

Last year, while I was team teaching science, my class explored a contact zone with the question Is a light wave or matter? After reading, experimenting, and interviewing experts, the class concluded that light is a wave that often behaves like matter. My students were astonished that even in physics, many important issues about which much evidence exists are still being debated and explored.

What was interesting about this experience is that the students did not have an *a priori* interest in understanding light. Through a lively introduction to the topic and humane instruction, we cultivated an interest in the topic, which became very keen on the part of our students. We also assisted them in the use of general scientific tools, such as observation and note taking, and of specific tools, such as how to play with and measure light with various optics and light bulbs. This increased the students' sense of both competence and agency as they manipulated tools and learned how to articulate operational definitions of various phenomena.

In exploring contact zones, my students are nearly all highly motivated. Unlike many assignments in which the teacher already knows the answer and the inquiry is fake, students see that knowledge must be created and a position must be taken. Motivation runs high, purpose is clear, and agency is foregrounded.

Make Reading Visible: Learning How to Read

Having a clear, relevant, and interesting purpose for reading is a necessary starting point. But it is also vital that students be assisted with the procedures (How) of reading particular kinds of texts for particular kinds of purposes. If we want students to know how to pursue and successfully complete specific kinds of reading tasks, then we need to make the general and task-specific processes of reading visible, we need to name particular tasks and what needs to be done to complete them, and we need to assist students to be able to do this kind of work.

In my own thinking, I have been compelled by the arguments of Smagorinsky and Smith (1992) that general processes of reading (such as summarizing, predicting, monitoring) are necessary but insufficient to successful reading of particular texts and the completion of particular tasks. If students are reading a genre such as satire or argument, there are many task-specific strategies they are unlikely to learn on their own. They need to be taught to recognize the need for these strategies and learn how to use them. I also agree with them that "genre" is most useful when conceived as sets of texts that make similar interpretive demands on readers. In this argument, poetry is not a genre at all, nor is nonfiction. Lyric poetry, or ironic monologue—sets of texts that require similar interpretive moves—would make up a genre and could be taught as texts that expect similar things of their readers.

During our unit on the use of sports, my students read sports narratives with which they required little assistance. But they also read a variety of autobiographies that required them to judge a narrator's reliability, and they read arguments that demanded they understand notions of evidence and warranting. We concluded by reading *Death of a Salesman* as we concerned ourselves with how Willie and Biff were influenced positively or negatively by notions from American sports. Reading a dramatic play has very special requirements, yet because our purpose was clear and motivation was high, and because I assisted students to recognize and use the necessary strategies, reading the play proved a success. Think about this: reading *Death of a Salesman* was a success with reluctant middle school readers. I'm almost afraid that I've stretched my credibility—but there you have it: when students are motivated and are assisted, they can extend their reach.

I need to emphasize, though, that I found it necessary to teach my students how to read such texts. To do so, I needed to make the demands and construction of such texts visible to them, and I needed to make visible how to respond in meaning-constructive ways to the codes of the text.

I modeled my own reading by using techniques such as the protocol, or "think aloud" (Newell, 1984); picture mapping, a variety of drama techniques (Wilhelm, 1996; Wilhelm & Edmiston, 1998); a technique called "symbolic story representation" (Enciso, 1996; Wilhelm, 1997); and stimulated recall (Bloom, 1954), a technique in which students watch videotapes of themselves creating artistic or dramatic responses to their reading and report what they were thinking and doing at the time that they created the response. I taught the students to use these techniques so that they could make their own reading visible and share their ways of reading with their classmates.

As students read particular kinds of texts around the contact zone theme, they not only explored the conceptual domain of the topic, they also explored and built knowledge of how to read particular kinds of texts. I worked to help students articulate and bring their knowledge forward by reflecting with them on what we were learning about how to read—both generally and in particular situations—and by keeping charts in front of the classroom that basically defined heuristics, or sets of reading strategies, that could be used while reading particular kinds of texts.

Interestingly, as we attempted to thoughtfully apply what we were learning and achieve significant, performance-based outcomes, students often used the techniques of composition, art, and drama to create hypermedia documents (Wilhelm & Friedemann, 1998), video documents, dramas, museum exhibits, petitions, social initiatives, or written arguments (Wilhelm & Edmiston, 1998). These became "knowledge artifacts" that could work in the real world. I have elsewhere written about the social projects that my students have taken up as part of and as a result of their reading agendas (Wilhelm, 1997; Wilhelm & Edmiston; Wilhelm & Friedemann). These have included campaigns to raise awareness of gender issues, historical explorations of civil rights issues through video documentary, local history projects, environmental initiatives, service to a senior citizen home, and many other projects like these. Knowledge, as Whitehead argued, is not "inert"; it begs to be put to use. Students want to be of use. They want to exercise agency, and if helped to do so, they will do so with gusto. Reading and writing are part of how we learn and work in the real world. Why not in school?

Thus, the "how" of reading becomes a way of translating what we are learning into social action. The techniques for making reading visible and our learning accountable become ways of making our knowledge visible to others and making our learning do work.

What to Read

The argument about what to read, particularly about what to read in school, has been raging for many years, since before Swift wrote *The Battle of the Books*. In America, the debate has been foregrounded at least since the Committee of Ten convened in the 1890s and has gained new impetus with the contributions of E. D. Hirsch's *Cultural Literacy*, Bloom's *The Closing of the American Mind*, the influence of Rosenblatt's transactional theory of literature, and others.

If I've made a convincing argument up to this point, the answer of what to read should now be clear: It depends! There is certainly no definitive canon or Top 100 list such as the kind put out recently by Bennett Cerf Jr. Students should read what helps them address the issues involved in contact zones of great relevance and significance. They should read the kinds of texts that speak most directly to these concerns. These texts will certainly include argument, various kinds of nonfiction (which have been relatively underused in schools, cf. Bamford and Kristo, 1997), satire, graphs, artifacts, informants, and always—yes, I say always—poetry, stories, and other kinds of texts considered to be literature. I say "always" because literature has always been about what matters most, and literature takes as its domain the exploration of what it means to struggle to be most fully wide awake and human in the world.

It used to be that the poet was considered to be the sage of the political and social world. By restoring literature to an exploration of human concerns, and by connecting it to the creation of knowledge artifacts and social action, I believe that we can make all reading—including the reading of literature—something that is not "stupid" at all, but interesting, intensely and movingly relevant, and compellingly necessary.

References

Bamford, R., & Kristo, J. (1998). *Making facts come alive: Choosing quality nonfiction literature*. Norwood, MA: Christopher-Gordon.

Bizzell, P. (1994). "Contact zones" and English studies. *College English, 56* (2), 163–69.

Bloom, B. (1954). The thought process of students in discussion. In S. J. French (Ed.), *Accent on teaching experiments in general education.* (pp. 23–46). New York: Harper and Brothers.

Enciso, P. (1996). Why engagement matters to Molly. *Reading and Writing Quarterly, 12* (1), 171–94.

Newell, G. (1984). Learning from writing in two content areas: A case study / protocol analysis. *Research in the Teaching of English, 18* (3), 265–87.

Pollack, W. (1998). *Real boys: Rescuing our sons from the myths of boyhood.* New York: Random House.

Postman, N. (1995). *The end of education: Redefining the value of school.* New York: Knopf.

Pratt, M. L. (1991). Arts of the contact zone. *Profession 91.* New York: MLA, 33–40.

Smagorinsky, P., & Smith, M. (1992). The nature of knowledge in composition and literary understanding: The question of specificity. *Review of Educational Research, 62* (3), 279–306.

Wilhelm, J. (1996). *Standards in practice, grades 6–8.* Urbana, IL: National Council of Teachers of English.

Wilhelm, J. (1997). *You gotta BE the book: Teaching engaged and reflective reading with adolescents.* New York: Teachers College Press.

Wilhelm, J., & Edmiston, B. (1998). *Imagining to learn: Inquiry, ethics, and integration through drama.* Portsmouth, NH: Heinemann.

Wilhelm, J., & Friedemann, P. (1998). *Hyperlearning: Where projects, inquiry, and technology meet.* York, ME: Stenhouse.

Jeffrey D. Wilhelm is currently an assistant professor at the University of Maine, where he teaches courses in middle and secondary level literacy. Wilhelm taught reading and the language arts at the middle and secondary levels for fifteen years. His interests include team teaching, co-constructing inquiry-driven curriculum with students, and pursuing teacher research. Most recently, he has been studying adolescent boys and their reading, their aspirations, and the school opportunities available to them for actualizing these aspirations. He works with local schools as part of the Adolescent Literacy project. He is also the director of two annual summer institutes: the Maine Writing Project and Technology as a Learning Tool. He is also active in Maine's Middle Level Education Institute, and he works with graduate students focusing on middle school and secondary literacy issues. Wilhelm is a recent recipient of the NCTE Promising Young Researcher Award (1995). He is currently working on *Boys and Books: Understanding the Literacy Crises of Boys and What We Can Do about It.*

2 From Hall Talk to Classroom Talk to Book Talk: Helping Struggling Readers Connect to Reading

Kylene Beers
University of Houston, Houston, Texas

Middle schoolers. If you teach them, you love them and then can't stand them. You find them to be mature and immature, responsible and irresponsible, childlike and adultlike, humorous and serious, spontaneous and methodical, respectful and irreverent. And that's all within first period. The good class.

They are an interesting lot, middle schoolers. They claim individuality yet strive to look like, dress like, sound like all around them. They claim independence yet won't go anywhere without a pack of friends following, leading, or just hanging close. They shut their bedroom doors and put up signs that say "No Parents" or "Keep Out" or "Friends Only" and then complain that parents don't care what they have to say. Their "I'm-on-top-of-the-world" attitudes can be shattered with the passing of a note, the exchange of a look, or the inability to find someone to sit with at lunch.

They drive us crazy, and they steal our hearts. Teachers of middle schoolers know that this group of young adolescents presents some of the most challenging teaching situations any adult could ever face—and some of the most rewarding. Most "HBC-ers" (Here By Choice, as one twenty-eight-year veteran of middle schools described herself) wouldn't dream of teaching any other age group. Those who discover that they don't have the patience or the energy or the interest to teach these kids generally get out fast. So what we end up with in the middle level are some of the most dynamic, most committed, most willing to learn, and most eager to teach educators I've ever seen. With that willingness comes a desire not only to reach those motivated students—those students so easy to teach—but also to reach the most difficult students, the students who seem not to care about learning or grades or moving on to high school and certainly not to college. We see those students walk the hall with a swagger and a smile and a "Yo" for friends and then walk into our classrooms and slump, sleep, and shut us out. "Is the air different?" one eighth-grade teacher asked me as she described the difference she saw in her struggling students in the hall and in the classroom. "What do you mean?" I asked. She replied in some detail:

> Well, out there, in the hall, they do everything I want them doing in my class. They ask questions, yell out responses, argue over who's right, make judgments, explain their positions, and show a real interest in what their peers have to say. But in here, it's like the dead zone. They become zombies who only answer my questions with blank stares or repetitions of my questions. They don't listen to one another, they don't answer one another, they don't ever explain their positions because they don't take a position. I want that energy they have out there brought in here. I'm thinking of moving my classroom into the hallway.

What creates that variance? Why the energy in the hall and the lethargy in the classroom? We've all seen that contrast and have wondered how the kid in the back row can be so sleepy in class and so lively in the hall. Natalie explained what she thinks the difference is all about:

> School, it be havin' two parts. Class time and hall time. Class time is where you discover what you can't do. Hall time is where you discover what you can do. Who you be hangin' with, who you be goin' with, who you be tight with. What's important in the halls, it ain't important in the class. In the class, it is about knowing stuff that don't mean anything, don't get you nowhere. But in the hall, it be about listenin' all the time so you know what be goin' on, and then when you know it, and you go it, and you tell it on to someone else and then they be thinkin' that you knowin' good stuff. And they like, "Cool" and then you be feelin' good so you be workin' harder at knowin' more.

Natalie, thirteen years old at the end of sixth grade, reads with some fluency and understanding books such as Arnold Lobel's *Frog and Toad Are Friends*. Those short, beginning-to-read chapter books are in no way similar to the literature, social studies, science, and math textbooks she must read for school. Nor do they reflect the difficulty of the trade books she reads for her language arts class. With her sixth-grade textbooks, Natalie is a dependent, disfluent reader. She lacks the strategies that would help her through difficult texts, and lacks the fluency that would allow her to move through texts with any sort of speed. She has given up on the thought that reading is about understanding. For her, reading is about finishing, about embarrassment, about failure.

So, Natalie walks into classrooms lacking the literacy ability that she needs to at least survive, if not thrive, in the classroom. Like all adolescents, Natalie will go to great lengths not to be laughed at, not to be "dumb-scum"—to use her language. Not knowing how to read well means for Natalie that she must decide that she doesn't want to know how to read well. That wall built, she has no reason to participate in class; thus, the slumping, sleeping, and slacking. When I described to Natalie her behavior in the hall and her behavior in the classroom and asked what really was creating such a difference, she quietly replied:

> I can't do it, can't do the readin'. After about 2nd grade it got, I don't know, it jus' got to bein' real hard. I be tryin' it for a while but the words, the words they jus' got harder and stuff and then they start puttin' me in these slow groups and everything there it was bein' so dumb like the teachers they was thinkin' that jus' 'cause we couldn't be readin' good we dumb and so she be always jus' askin' us real dumb like questions and then I jus' start bein' angry and stuff. . . . It's the readin'. You can't do that, you can't do school. Might as well jus' be checkin' out.

Natalie's right. It is the reading. When kids make it to middle school as poor readers, they've got more problems than simply not being able to comprehend a text. They are smart enough to have figured out that school is about literacy and when you aren't literate, then you just don't fit. Not fitting in for middle schoolers is the kiss of death. But they don't have the option of not attending; therefore, when they attend, they just create their own rules. The purpose of school isn't what goes on in the classes, but instead, what goes on in the halls.

Connecting Kids to Literacy

To reconnect those students to what goes on in classrooms means first convincing them that what's happening in the classrooms is relevant to their lives. For some middle schoolers the simple reminder that "you need this for high school" or even "this will help you in college" is very pertinent to their lives and that's all we need to say to get them to do most anything. But those reasons aren't relevant for kids who don't see high school or college in their futures, for kids who barely see beyond a day. Instead, those kids need "hall talk" in the classroom. They need what Natalie was describing—talk about things that matter to them here, now, today. Talk about things that help them make sense of who they are. That doesn't mean our classrooms must become venues for finding out who's going out with whom. But it does mean we have to listen to the topics that interest them and work from those topics.

As literature teachers, we have the ability to share books that address topics that appeal to them. That means books with topics covering everything from friendship to first loves, parents to pets, giving up to going on. Our poorest readers deserve our best books. They've had years of workbooks and worksheets (material that is often of little interest to them) and classroom anthologies (literature that is often beyond their independent reading ability). Now, they need some time with books that capture their interests yet meet their independent reading levels. One way to meet those needs is by grouping books thematically. For instance, with the theme "Courage through the Tough Times" students are introduced to several books. After listening to book talks for each book, each student chooses a book that most appeals to his or her interests and best meets his or her reading ability. As a result, during this unit, struggling readers might choose Scott O'Grady's *Basher Five-Two* while more accomplished readers might choose Gary Paulsen's *Hatchet* or Martha Southgate's *Another Way to Dance* while even more skilled readers might select Robert Cormier's *The Chocolate War* or Harper Lee's *To Kill a Mockingbird*. Readers of these various books come together to discuss questions such as

> What makes a person courageous?
>
> Can a person be courageous and afraid at the same time?
>
> Which character in your book showed the most courage? What did that person do that you considered courageous?
>
> Which character in your book are you most like? Most unlike?
>
> What passage gave you the most insight into your character?
>
> What's a trait in one of the characters from the book you read you'd most like to see in yourself?
>
> What does this book tell you about living in today's world?
>
> Is courage important?
>
> What does it mean when we aren't courageous?

By grouping books thematically, readers who choose *Basher Five-Two*, *Hatchet*, or *Another Way to Dance* have as much to say as readers who choose *The Chocolate War* and *To Kill a Mockingbird*. Derek, a fifteen-year-old eighth grader, actively participated for the first time in a discussion group after reading *Basher Five-Two*. The group's discussion lasted two days as students talked passionately about courage—theirs, others, and the characters in their books. As the discussions began to slow, students then wrote about courage. Some chose to write poems; some wrote reports about real people who did courageous things; others wrote descriptive papers. Derek, when asked to explain what type of paper he wrote, answered, "Don't know. Just wrote down what I wanted to say." I think he said a lot:

> I read *Basher Five-Two*. It was a good book. It was about how this fighter pilot got shot down behind enamy lines and had to survieve by useing survieval skills like eating bugs and diging a hole he could stay in at night and he has ants all over him but could'nt move or make any noises because the enamy soltiers where evarywere. He had to have faith that his troop would come back in to get him and save him. I would like to have the same fathe that he has got because I am down behind enemy lines to. I got things that make me want to cry but if I cry I get puntched and told I'm a crybaby sissy. He has alot of curage because in the tuf times he kept on going. I keep on going alot of times to. But how long would his curage have lasted if noone had come to get him? That's what I want to no. How long does you're curage last when the troops don't come?

Derek connected with this unit because he has lots of questions about courage. Just as Natalie's notion that hall talk is important because it's about her daily life, the classroom talk about courage became important to Derek for the same reason. So, creating real connections to struggling readers' lives is necessary. What they read must be meaningful to them. I want to be clear here that I believe that all middle schoolers—avid readers, dormant readers (kids who like to read but just have put it aside for the time being), reluctant readers, and struggling readers—would benefit from a thematically based literature curriculum. The reality, though, is different. I've seen time and time again that some kids will read just because we tell them to (even if they don't see an immediate connection to the text) while others won't read unless that connection to their lives is immediate and powerful.

Selecting the Right Books

The problem with choosing a single book for a heterogeneous class is that the text might be too difficult a read for some of the students and probably won't appeal to the interests of all the students. What do struggling readers do with our required readings but once again face a text that is generally too difficult and therefore confirms their notion that reading isn't for them. Thematic groupings of books allow all levels of readers to participate, to become a community of readers. Yes, we can be a community of readers as we read different books. The community is established as readers discuss the commonalties and differences in their books. It means we've spent some time thinking about the novels students might read, making sure the various books will appeal to the various reading abilities that are in our classrooms, and coming up with topics that connect the books. Figure 2.1 offers two additional themes and books for those themes.

Here are two thematic units with book titles and discussion starters. Books that are most accessible for struggling readers are indicated with an asterisk. Remember, a student's interest and motivation in reading a particular book is always more important than the book's vocabulary or syntax. Also remember that all the books listed for these units do not have to be used. As you select books, try to keep boys and girls as main characters balanced. Also, try to offer enough books so that you appeal to the ability levels of all readers in your classroom.

Winning against the Odds

Another Way to Dance. Martha Southgate
Catherine Called Birdy. Karen Cushman
Crews: Gang Members Talk to Maria Hinojosa. Maria Hinojosa
I Am Regina. Sally Keehn*
If I Forget, You Remember. Carol Lynch Williams
Into Thin Air: A Personal Account of the Mount Everest Disaster. Jon Krakauer
Kids at Work: Lewis Hine and the Crusade against Child Labor. Russell Freedman
Mieko and the Fifth Treasure. Eleanor Coerr*
Sadako and the Thousand Paper Cranes. Eleanor Coerr*
Send Me Down a Miracle. Han Nolan
Under the Blood-Red Sun. Graham Salisbury*
Words by Heart. Ouida Sebestyn

Discussion Starters:
    What makes some situations overwhelming and others manageable? What do you do when you face a seemingly overwhelming situation? What is it that makes some people keep going, keep trying even when success seems impossible, while other people give up? Why do some people constantly shout "Not fair" when things get tough while others just look for ways to accomplish whatever they are trying to do? What do you do when you encounter unfair situations? What do you do when you encounter tough situations? What does it mean to win something? Can you win without coming in first? How can you turn a losing situation into a winning one?

continued on next page

Figure 2.1. Thematic Units and Discussion Starters

Figure 2.1 continued

What tough situations did the characters face in the books you read? Was there anything unfair about those situations? How did the characters react to those situations. What does the sentence "I will not be beat by defeat" mean to you? What might it mean to a character in one of the books you read? Which victories are more important to you, easy ones or hard fought ones? What were the victories and defeats your characters faced? Which do you think were most important to them? What can you say about winning against the odds after having read your book(s)?

Turning Points

Driver's Ed. Caroline Cooney
Goodbye, Vietnam. Gloria Whelan
Hard Time: A Real Life Look at Juvenile Crime and Violence. Janet Bode
Kissing Doorknobs. Terry Spencer Hesser
Leaving Home. Hazel Rochman and Darlene Z. McCambell, editors
Nothing but the Truth: A Documentary Novel. Avi
Out of the Dust. Karen Hesse
P.S. Longer Letter Later. Paula Danziger and Ann M. Martin
Riding Freedom. Pam Munoz Ryan*
Saving Shiloh. Phyllis Reynolds
Soldier's Heart. Gary Paulsen
Tangerine. Edward Bloor
The Giver. Lois Lowry
The Iron Dragon Never Sleeps. Stephen Krensky*
The Printer's Apprentice. Stephen Krensky*
The Slave Dancer. Paula Fox
The Witch of Blackbird Pond. Elizabeth George Speare

Discussion Starters:

Spend some time reflecting on tough decisions you've had to make. What made these decisions tough? How much were you influenced by what your friends or family would say about your decision? Why are we influenced by our peers when it comes to making decisions? Should we pay attention to that influence? Can you identify the point at which you finally made the decision? Would you call the decision a turning point? If so, what did it turn you away from and toward? After reading one or more of the following books, can you identify turning points these characters faced? What did you learn about decision making, peer influence, and the importance of turning points from these characters and/or their situations? Discuss the following statement with some friends and explain whether you agree or disagree. Use situations from your life and from one of the novels to support your position: "Turning points are difficult because the outcomes are also generally difficult."

Developing Reading Tools

But in most middle schools, students do not spend their entire English periods reading trade books of choice. Literature anthologies and required novels are a part of the curriculum in many, if not most, schools. That means giving those struggling readers tools for getting through difficult texts so that as they move through those texts they are on their way to becoming independent readers. That means they must learn and then internalize the *strategies* they need to comprehend difficult texts, the *fluency* they need to move through the many pages they must read with any sort of speed, the *vocabulary* they need to understand concepts presented in literature and content area books, and the *concentration* they need to stay focused for more than one paragraph (or for some, one sentence!) at a time. Without these tools, students often stumble when they encounter challenging texts. They become either what I call "read-on-through readers"—those kids who just keep their eyes moving over words, lines, pages from beginning to end without any effort to make those words make any type of sense— or they become "stop, look, and wait readers"—the other kids who at the first word, first line, or first concept they fail to grasp immediately stop, look at us, and wait for us to explain to them what they ought to figure out on their own. Neither strategy creates an independent reader.

Can we help those struggling readers? Can we create independence after so many years of dependence? Can we encourage an interest in reading that died in part because of a lack of ability to read? Yes. But to do so means knowing comprehension strategies, vocabulary strategies, and motivational strategies that work specifically for struggling secondary readers. Figure 2.2 contains a list of the strategies I've found to be most helpful and titles of books and articles you can read to help you learn more about those strategies.

Really helping struggling readers means giving them an opportunity to read within their reading reach for at least part of the class time (thus thematic groupings of books), and we must give them the strategies they need to help them through those more difficult texts. I've found that merely giving them the strategies won't work because these kids have decided reading isn't for them; on the other hand, offering them only easy-to-read books also won't work because creating an interest without creating the ability to handle more difficult reading is not fair to the students. We've got to do both: create an interest *and* teach the skills.

Natalie really is right. School is about reading and when you can't do it, you really do feel as if you might as well check out. And Derek is right as well—the question to ask about courage is how long can you stay courageous when the rescue troops don't seem to be around. I don't begin to assume that I understand all of Natalie's and Derek's enemies; however, I do understand one of them: the inability to read well. As

Comprehension strategies I have found to be very effective include the following: Say Something, Think Aloud, Retells, and Text Reformulation. Read more about each of these strategies in the following publications:

Tierney, R., Readence, J., & Dishner, E. (1995). *Reading strategies and practices: A compendium.* Boston, MA: Allyn & Bacon.

Beers, K., & Samuels, B. (Eds.). (1998). *Into focus: Understanding and creating middle school readers.* Norwood, MA: Christopher-Gordon.

Brown, H., & Cambourne, B. (1987). *Read and retell: A strategy for the whole-language/natural learning classroom.* Portsmouth, NH: Heinemann.

Excellent vocabulary strategies to use include vocabulary maps and vocabulary trees. Read more about these strategies in the following books:

Allen, J. (1999). *Words, words, words: Teaching vocabulary in grades 4–12.* York, ME: Stenhouse.

Beers, K., & Samuels, B. (Eds.). (1998). *Into focus: Understanding and creating middle school readers.* Norwood, MA: Christopher-Gordon.

Blachowicz, C., & Fisher, P. (1996). *Teaching vocabulary in all classrooms.* Englewood Cliffs, NJ: Merrill.

Motivating reluctant and struggling readers is difficult. For information about specific motivational strategies, try the following sources:

Beers, K. (1996). No time, no interest, no way! Part I. *School Library Journal, 42* (2), 30–33.

Beers, K. (1996). No, time, no interest, no way! Part II. *School Library Journal, 42* (3), 110–13.

Krogness, M. (1995). *Just teach me, Mrs. K.: Talking, reading, and writing with resistant adolescent learners.* Portsmouth, NH: Heinemann.

Wilhelm, J. (1997). *You gotta BE the book: Teaching engaged and reflective reading with adolescents.* New York: Teachers College Press.

For information about the use of audiobooks with reluctant readers, read the following:

Beers, K. (1998). Listen while you read: Struggling readers and audiobooks. *School Library Journal, 44* (4), 30–35.

For more information about the development of response-centered classrooms, try the following sources:

Atwell, N. (1998). *In the middle: New understandings about writing, reading, and learning.* Portsmouth, NH: Boynton/Cook.

Beers, K., & Samuels, B. (Eds.). (1998). *Into focus: Understanding and creating middle school readers.* Norwood, MA: Christopher-Gordon.

Probst, R. (1988). *Response and analysis: Teaching literature in junior and senior high school.* Portsmouth, NH: Heinemann.

Rief, L. (1992). *Seeking diversity: Language arts with diversity.* Portsmouth, NH: Boynton/Cook.

Figure 2.2. A List of Comprehension Strategies to Aid Struggling Readers

struggling readers, Natalie and Derek are being as courageous as they can be while waiting for the rescue troops to arrive. They have their defenses in place and are taking all sorts of evasive measures. Our job is to get there before they give up and check out, to convince them that we are the rescue troops and not the enemy, to show them that talk about books—classroom talk—can be as relevant as hall talk. It's a tough challenge, but one I believe middle school teachers can handle.

References

Cormier, R. (1974). *The chocolate war*. New York: Bantam Doubleday Dell.

Lee, H. (1982). *To kill a mockingbird*. New York: Warner Books.

Lobel, A. (1970). *Frog and toad are friends*. New York: HarperCollins.

O'Grady, S. with M. French. (1997). *Basher five-two*. New York: Bantam Doubleday Dell.

Paulsen, G. (1987). *Hatchet*. New York: Bradbury Press.

Southgate, M. (1996). *Another way to dance*. New York: Bradbury Press.

Kylene Beers is a veteran middle school teacher who has turned her commitment to helping struggling readers into the major focus of her research, writing, speaking, and teaching. Now an assistant clinical professor at the University of Houston, she continues to spend much of her time in classrooms collaborating with teachers on developing strategies for helping students become skilled and engaged readers of literary and informational texts. Beers is editor for *Voices from the Middle* and the NCTE senior high booklist, *Books for You*. She is co-editor of the widely read professional text *Into Focus: Understanding and Creating Middle School Readers* and former co-editor of the NCTE middle school/junior high booklist, *Your Reading*. Beers serves on the review boards for *English Journal* and the *ALAN Review*. She frequently presents at state and national conferences.

3 Teaching Literature through Thematic Units

Mary Santerre
The Village School, Houston, Texas

As a middle school teacher of language arts, my job is quite challenging. How do I cover the literary elements of my curriculum guide, allow my students flexibility in their reading choices, use the anthology provided by the school, and manage to instill a passion for reading in my middle school students? The key, in large part, is the format I use to organize the content of the middle school reading workshop: thematic units.

Definition of and Rationale for Thematic Units

The term *thematic* suggests a variety of ways to organize content. One possible way to develop the thematic unit is a topic such as relationships or conflicts. Another way to build a thematic unit is based on a literary theme such as initiation and maturation. In our reading workshop, I have chosen to use a blend of both topical and literary themes. In the first quarter I use a thematic unit called "Courage under Fire," which I base on the theme of initiation and maturation. In the fourth quarter, though, I use a thematic grouping called "Voices from the Past," a topic-related unit. It emphasizes a variety of voices from many genres that cause us to reflect about the past. Those voices are as divergent as the autobiographical voice of Elie Wiesel in *Night* and the fictional voice of Rebecca in Daphne DuMaurier's *Rebecca*.

Perhaps the question I am most often asked is, "Why don't you just teach from your anthology and throw in a few novels along the way?" Thematic grouping allows me to offer a wide variety of reading possibilities that support a major tenant of my philosophy as a reading teacher: allow as much variety and choice in the reading curriculum as possible. In the unit "Courage under Fire," I can select readings that deal with the ideas of characters coming of age and enduring the trials of growing up. I can make historical ties with my social studies interdisciplinary team and choose the core novel to coincide with the time period. My class studies the protagonist Adam in Howard Fast's

April Morning; this focus coincides with the history department's teaching of the Revolutionary War. The literary theme also allows the study of current events in magazines and newspapers. I really enjoy sharing Captain Scott O'Grady's experience of being shot down in Bosnia as an example of "fire" of the most severe psychological and physical types. The theme of initiation and maturation in "Courage under Fire" enables the students to choose almost any book in young adult literature for individual reading. Last year, students read of the courage under fire of fictional young adult characters from Caroline Cooney's *Driver's Ed* to Melba Beals's own real-life courage under fire in her book *Warriors Don't Cry.* Thematic grouping allows for the inclusion of nonprint text as well. During the first quarter, students see clips of *Dead Poets' Society* and *The Crucible* and are asked to examine the initiation and maturation theme within the context of the films. As part of the beginning of the course, the class members share their own stories of courage and maturation, which helps to establish a sense of community in our reading and writing workshop.

Getting Started with Thematic Units

Colleagues often ask the very concrete question, "If I decide to use thematic groupings, how in the world do I get started?" As an introduction to others who would like to implement thematic units, I have prepared a list that might be helpful.

- Carefully read your curriculum guide, checking objectives and skills.
- Peruse the available literature.
- Determine a budget.
- Make a chart to determine teaching units.
- Formulate thematic units.
    Examples
    "Courage under Fire"
    "Just beneath the Surface Lies the Truth"
    "Destiny Defined: Lives That Have Made a Difference"
    "Voices from the Past"
- Determine placement of major literature selections.
- Determine core novel (if possible).
- Decide whether to include choice selections.

- Arrange composition modes and topics to complement literature.
- Analyze grammar, mechanics, and usage needs to fit scope and
  sequence.

Planning the Course Using Thematic Units

I have found that as I move from school to school and use different
curriculum guides, I make constant revisions on my "working plans."
The working of the thematic units is a process that I constantly evaluate
and revise—from year to year, week to week, and day to day. I make
notes throughout each unit, and as the year progresses I frequently
make changes to my "original plan," adding and deleting as necessary
and adjusting the selection of choice readings. The core novels will
change from year to year, but I usually decide on them at the beginning
of each year. Each quarter is roughly broken down in the following way:

- Three weeks on core novel, poetry, and film
- Three weeks on anthology materials, particularly short stories
  and nonfiction
- Three weeks on choice books

Returning to the challenge of my job as middle school teacher—
getting it all done—I am positive it never all gets done. However,
thematic units provide the opportunity to get as much of the "all" done
as possible: using the anthology, meeting the requirements of the
curriculum guide, allowing choice and variety in the reading selections,
and insuring an immediacy and relevancy of materials such as current
articles, poetry, film, and so on. Using thematic groupings provides
response and analysis in a larger framework of choice for my students.
I offer choices that are relevant and important to my middle school
readers, giving them moments of joy and passion.

References

Beals, M. P. (1995). *Warriors don't cry: A searing memoir of the battle to integrate Little Rock's Central High.* New York: Washington Square Press.

Beers, K., & Samuels, B. (Eds.). (1998). *Into focus: Understanding and creating middle school readers.* Norwood, MA: Christopher-Gordon.

Cooney, C. (1994). *Driver's ed.* New York: Delacorte Press.

Du Maurier, D. (1965). *Rebecca.* New York: Doubleday.

Fast, H. M. (1970). *April morning.* New York: Noble and Noble.

Moss, J. (1994). *Using literature in the middle grades: A thematic approach.* Norwood, MA: Christopher-Gordon.

Wiesel, E. (1960). *Night.* New York: Avon Books.

Mary Santerre teaches at the Village School, a private school in west Houston, Texas. Santerre has taught English for nineteen years, the last ten focusing "in the middle" with eighth graders. She received her B.A. in English at Houston Baptist University and her M.A. at the Bread Loaf School of English at Middlebury College. She has attended both the New Jersey Writing Project and the Greater Houston Area Writing Project.

4 Nonfiction and Young Readers

Robert C. Small Jr.
Radford University, Radford, Virginia

Nonfiction. "Who cares! The very title for the genre itself tells us what it is *not* but not what it is: It is a "non" something. It is as if poetry were called "nonprose," or drama, "nonnovel," or you or I were termed "non-turtles."

Indeed, a few writers of nonfiction have sought a better term. Some have suggested "informational prose"; that name, however—besides suggesting writing of exhausting dreariness—really only applies to one small part of what is generally lumped under "nonfiction."

So what is it? In fact, nonfiction comprises a diverse array of literary types—including biography, autobiography, travel narratives, descriptions of historical events, essays (a multidimensional type in itself), and many other literary genres.

Unfortunately, teachers of English language arts rarely see nonfiction as aesthetic, probably because they have not studied nonfiction as a literary form. Look into the course listings for the English department in any university catalogue, and you will find courses devoted to Shakespeare and Chaucer, to the short story and the epic poem, to twentieth-century American writers. You will probably not, however, find a course devoted to nonfiction. English majors planning to be teachers do study some nonfiction, where nonfiction is not studied for itself but rather to illustrate the major writers of the type from the literary period under consideration or to illustrate the thought of the educated people of the time. In a course on poetry or the short story or the novel, the class will examine the characteristics of the form and its development over time, perhaps even look at the decisions a writer makes as a work is conceived and developed. Nonfiction universally gets no such attention.

A similar version of this essay entitled "Non-fiction and the Teenage Reader" appeared in the fall 1991 issue of *Virginia English Bulletin*.

Teenagers and Nonfiction

Teenage readers gravitate to nonfiction, especially nonfiction that deals with their interests or that looks at teenagers caught up in situations or problems they can relate to. Betty Carter and Dick Abrahamson point out that we often see young readers as falling into the following categories, among others: those who say they like to read, those who say they can read but do not, and those who have poor reading skills and rarely read. This examination of those students who say they can read but do not has revealed that many of them do read a fair amount. What they read, however, is nonfiction, and they do not see such reading as reading. They are condemned by themselves as nonreaders because they read books related to their interests and because they read books other than novels or poems or the other literary types praised by their teachers. What teachers call reading leads these students to label themselves "nonreaders." And that, it seems, is where they get that odd view of themselves: from their teachers.

Carter and Abrahamson also point out that young readers will often read works of nonfiction that, by conventional measures, would be far too difficult for them. They will struggle with a text that deals with hunting dogs, the life of Magic Johnson, and other interests because those books tap into their *interests*.

Sources for Teachers of Nonfiction

Although there remain far more guides for the use of fiction and poetry in classes than for nonfiction, in the last few years, three especially helpful such guides have appeared.

Betty Carter of Texas Woman's University and Richard Abrahamson of the University of Houston describe the purpose of *Nonfiction for Young Adults: From Delight to Wisdom* (1990) this way:

> We hope this book will begin to negate the prejudice against nonfiction. We hope to show the literary qualities of nonfiction as well as to define its importance for young adults. We suggest that the vital element nonfiction lacks is professional attention. Since we know that young adults read nonfiction and that nonfiction volumes make up an average of two-thirds to three-fourths of most library holdings, it's time to take a serious look at the genre. (pp. ix–x)

They go on to trace the history of the terms *nonfiction* and *fiction:* "In our reading we've come to respect nonfiction. We've encountered authors we've grown to admire, titles deserving to be read, and young adults seeking reading guidance. We hope that through this book we can extend some of these pleasures to you" (1990, p. xiii). Using those goals as a starting place, Carter and Abrahamson begin by examining the question of interest and, based on a review of reading research studies, they make the following statement: "Young adults read nonfiction; this interest in nonfiction crosses ability levels; and on the whole, teenage boys tend to read more nonfiction than teenage girls" (p. 3).

With those claims in mind, the authors explore the research that has led them to these conclusions. Next, they examine what they call "Pleasure versus Curriculum," that is, when and what do students read for enjoyment and when and what for class assignments and other such matters? They conclude with a look at the roles of librarians and teachers:

> Merely requiring young adults to read widely or forcing books on them will not automatically turn them into lifetime readers. But introducing a variety of books in classrooms, booktalks, and curriculum-related activities will begin to. Of course none of these tools will ever replace the one-to-one relationship between teachers and librarians and the teenagers they work with. Understanding the nuances of their interests and possessing the knowledge to match these with appropriate reading material are the most powerful tools teachers and librarians have for positively influencing a young adult's reading. (1990, p. 14)

Having established that interest in nonfiction exists and therefore needs further development, the authors turn to the question of selection, specifically the standards appropriate for determining the quality of a work of nonfiction. They divide this discussion into five chapters: "Accuracy," "Content," "Style," "Organization," and "Format."

Standards for judging works of nonfiction are not nearly as widely known among teachers of the English language arts, and these sections provide an invaluable resource for making wise judgments. They also suggest approaches that teachers might take in helping them guide their students in the exploration of how nonfiction is written, what choices its authors must make as they approach that writing, and what to look for in evaluating an individual work.

The authors conclude with a chapter entitled "Uses," in which they provide strategies that teachers and librarians can use within their programs to involve works of nonfiction. Under the heading "Point of View" they propose that students look at the ways in which different authors of nonfiction have explored and presented essentially the same topic, event, person, and so on. They use the Vietnam War as an example.

Between each of the chapters dealing with the nature and uses of nonfiction, Carter and Abrahamson include interviews with authors of nonfiction for young readers. They interview the authors Lee J. Ames, Milton Meltzer, Laurence Pringle, Brent Ashabranner, James Cross Giblin, and Daniel and Susan Cohen. The resulting interviews produce insightful commentaries by the authors on such matters as the art and craft of writing nonfiction, their purposes for doing such writing, and the nature of the teenage world.

In *The Best Years of Their Lives: A Resource Guide for Teenagers in Crisis*, (1992) Stephanie Zvirin, of *Booklist*, has prepared an extensive annotated bibliography of works of nonfiction that deal with problems teenage readers face. She includes a sample of related fiction as well.

In her introduction, she tells us that the lives of teenagers in this country have become dangerous, threatened by disease, suicide, poverty. But she says, "The Publishing industry has . . . reacted" (1992, p. viii). As Zvirin explains, nonfiction works that help teenagers examine the problems they face have grown rapidly in number:

1. They provide young adults with a sense of what they have in common with others their age, whether that be an unplanned pregnancy, an abusive parent, or simply pimples on their face.

2. They provide background information and useful suggestions for more confident handling of situations that occur in daily life, such as dating or sharing a room with a brother or sister.

3. They help teenagers determine life choices and adjust to the consequences of decision making.

4. They inform teens about the physical and psychological changes that come with adolescence. (p. viii)

With that governing set of purposes in mind, Zvirin explores, through brief introductory essays and short but comprehensive annotations, books that explore nine broad categories of teenage concerns: families, school, self, drugs and alcohol, sexual violence, health, sexuality, marriage and pregnancy, and death.

Typically, the annotations consist of half a page or less of description; however, Zvirin packs into them an extensive amount of detail and assessment of each book. And she does not hesitate to point out weaknesses in some of the books. In these annotations, she also suggests an age range for the readers to whom the book will appeal.

In addition to the annotations, the author has included a number of essays by or interviews with several of the authors of the books she has selected for inclusion. These authors include such widely read writers as Eda Leshan, Lynda Madaras, and Janet Bode.

Reproductions of the covers of some of the books as well as pictures of the authors who are interviewed make the book visually interesting, as do quotes pulled out from the texts of some of the books under review.

At the end of each topical section, Zvirin includes brief annotations of works of fiction that, in the context of teenage lives, deal with the same issue or problem. These annotations are much shorter than those of the nonfiction works: the emphasis of the book is clearly on nonfiction.

The author ends the book with a filmography, in which she very briefly annotates films and videos that relate to the issues around which she has organized the text.

Teenagers read nonfiction. They read it to learn about their lives, their world, their interests. Often nonfiction is all they will read. *The Best Years of Their Lives* is an invaluable guide to the best current nonfiction that explores the problems that teenagers face. Well-written, effectively organized, it should be in every library and every classroom in America.

A third recent publication by Evelyn B. Freeman and Diane Goetz Person, *Using Nonfiction Trade Books in the Elementary Classroom: From Ants to Zeppelins* (1992), provides help for classroom teachers who wish to use nonfiction with their students. This book was produced by the Committee on Using Nonfiction in the Elementary Language Arts Classroom. As is true of the other books reviewed in this article, this text attempts to define "nonfiction."

> We have struggled in our committee with the term *nonfiction*. Some prefer this term since it represents the generally accepted Dewey decimal classification of the books we are discussing. Others, however, take umbrage with the term and feel it connotes an inferior relationship to fiction. They would substitute the term *informational books* since it is this kind of book, along with biography, that we are discussing. (p. vii)

Despite their problem with defining the focus of their book, the authors present us with an excellent guide to nonfiction books for children and how they might be used in the curriculum.

The book is divided into three sections: "Understanding the Genre of Nonfiction," "Linking Nonfiction to the Elementary Curriculum," and "Finding a Place for Nonfiction in the Elementary Classroom." These main sections of the book reflect the problem that nonfiction presents for English language arts teachers: a lack of understanding of the genre, a curriculum that has not included nonfiction, and a failure on the part of teachers to understand both the role of nonfiction in children's reading and strategies to explore nonfiction with young readers. The authors set out to correct these problems, and they do so wonderfully well.

In the first section, "Understanding the Genre of Nonfiction," Russell Freeman, author of nonfiction for young readers, says this of nonfiction:

> Someone else has said that fiction is a pack of lies in pursuit of the truth. As a corollary, I suppose you could say that nonfiction is a pack of facts in pursuit of the truth. Unfortunately, facts can't always be trusted. Facts can be unreliable, misleading, ambiguous, or slippery. (Freeman & Person, 1992, p. 2)

He then explores the problem of the factual truth of books labeled "nonfiction" and the essential truth of works labeled "fiction." In this section, other writers of nonfiction for children explore their approaches to creating such books, and two librarians look at trends in the publishing of nonfiction.

In the second section, the authors look at the literary elements of nonfiction, science, and social studies books for children; strategies for using nonfiction, including reading aloud, discussions, writing nonfiction; and the relation of nonfiction and children's artistic creations.

The third section of *Using Nonfiction Trade Books in the Elementary Classroom* (Freeman & Person, 1992) focuses on various ways in which teachers have used nonfiction in their classrooms. Judith Keck, for example, describes a unit she has found successful: "In an author study, students examine all available books written by a single author, read widely from this collection of books, and explore the author's themes, topics, writing style, and format of published books" (p. 123). She goes on to describe her article as providing "a process for selecting an author, gathering materials, preparing for the study, involving students in reading, extending students' reading, and grading and evaluating students' work" (p. 123).

In "Using Information Books to Develop Reference Skills," Jean Greenlaw explores how the natural curiosity of young readers, when confronted by topics such as animals and the solar system, combined with innovative activities, can give research the excitement that some adults have but few children have felt.

With a rich and varied exploration of the roles that nonfiction can play in the elementary classroom—in reading study to be sure, but also science, social studies, expository writing, creative writing, and the many other dimensions of the elementary curriculum—*Using Nonfiction Trade Books in the Elementary Classroom* proves that nonfiction can go well beyond mere reading for information to be a major component of the curriculum.

Nonfiction, despite the negative quality of its name, may well be the most popular form of literature for today's young readers. Offering great diversity of subject, approach, viewpoint, and style, the body of nonfiction available for young readers is rich and provides something for every student. By familiarizing ourselves with our students' interests and with the nonfiction that is available, we can introduce into the literature program an excitement and intensity that is often lacking for students who want to read about the real world of their interests, problems, and concerns. Using guidebooks such as those reviewed in this article, we can explore with our students both the content and the aesthetic qualities of the works we read together and those we share with each other.

References

Carter, B., & Abrahamson, R. F. (1990). *Nonfiction for young adults: From delight to wisdom*. Phoenix: Oryx Press.

Zvirin, S. (1992). *The best years of their lives: A resource guide for teenagers in crisis*. Chicago: American Library Association.

Freeman, E. B., & Person, D. G. (1992). *Using nonfiction trade books in the elementary classroom: From ants to zeppelins*. Urbana, IL: National Council of Teachers of English.

Robert C. Small Jr. is dean of the College of Education and Human Development and professor of educational studies at Radford University. He has served as president of ALAN, co-editor of the *ALAN Review*, chair of the Conference on English Education, and co-editor of the *Virginia English Bulletin*. He chaired the NCTE Teacher Preparation and Certification Committee that prepared the *Guidelines for the Preparation of Teachers of English Language Arts*. He has written about young adult literature for *English Journal, Adolescent Literature as a Complement to the Classics, Volumes I and II*, and the *ALAN Review* and has presented workshops on literature for young readers at the conferences of NCTE, IRA, ALA, and at a number of conferences of NCTE state affiliates. His works on censorship have appeared in publications of NCTE, IRA, ALA, several books, and NCTE affiliate journals.

5 Literature and Lessons of the Holocaust: Theory and Practice

Marlene B. Hartstein
Montgomery County Schools, Rockville, Maryland

Karen Zelde Schejtman Sultan
Montgomery County Schools, Rockville, Maryland

Often because of one story, or one book, or one person, we are able to make a different choice, a choice for humanity.

—Elie Wiesel, *The Courage to Care*

In a world of increasing racial, ethnic, and religious hostility, the story of the Holocaust is an important tool to help children understand the implications of hatred. In 1993, these considerations led the National Council of Teachers of English to affirm that "students should read and discuss literature on genocide and intolerance within an historically accurate framework, with special emphasis on primary materials" (Goldberg, 1995, p. 104). Middle school English teachers have the opportunity to use young adult literature of the Holocaust to prepare "caring ethical individual(s), [who are] able to recognize that there is good and bad, and that it is possible and important to tell the difference" (Carnegie Council on Adolescent Development, 1989, p. 15).

What can prepare a teacher to face the particular paradoxes and ironies of teaching Holocaust literature? How can a teacher guide the reading of stories that can hardly be told, yet must be told? How does a teacher design lessons to answer unanswerable questions, to show how language can mask as well as reveal, and to lead a class to approach the core of evil in hopes of discovering the essence of goodness?

There are no simplistic answers to explain such complex historical events as the Holocaust. Certainly, there is no answer to a common question, "How could people do such a thing?" In the face of such questions, teachers may take heart and courage from the words of Moche the Beadle (quoted in *Night*), who believed that "every question possessed a power that did not lie in the answer" (Mahle, 1985, p. 84).

How does an English teacher, though, start to select the right books for the classroom? What strategies and guidelines see a class through reading some of the darkest and brightest chapters in history?

Materials

The themes inherent in young adult literature of the Holocaust address the classic themes English teachers regularly teach, and ones that young adults confront in their daily lives: identity, peer pressure, conformity, justice, coming of age, friendship, loyalty, prejudice, moral choices, and survival. The genre is likewise all-encompassing and familiar: poetry, fiction, biography, autobiography, drama, and so on. Literature of the Holocaust has its own classics, for example, *Anne Frank: The Diary of a Young Girl*, *Night*, and *I Never Saw Another Butterfly*. Also, many new works stand out, for example, *I Have Lived a Thousand Years* and *Light from the Yellow Star: A Lesson of Love from the Holocaust*. *Friedrich*, *The Devil's Arithmetic* and *Number the Stars* span reading, maturity, and interest levels; and picture books such as *Rose Blanche* make good read-alouds for a shared experience. The allegory of *Terrible Things* provides a simple beginning for a study.

Criteria for selection are easily recognizable: quality works that are age-appropriate, in which the history is accurate and the characters authentic; and stories that elicit respect and understanding and allow readers to draw their own conclusions. A short guide from the United States Holocaust Memorial Museum (available for free), *Teaching about the Holocaust*, provides an annotated bibliography as well as vocabulary, a time line of history, and a list of other resources.

Strategies for Teaching the Holocaust

A review of history, establishing a theoretical base, provides a strong introduction to Holocaust literature and will inform and set a reflective tone. Teachers may first want to present Allport's Five Levels of Prejudice:

Name calling: the stereotyping of an entire group

Isolation: the separation of the group from society

Discrimination: legal isolation

Physical attack

Extermination

The teacher can then move to reviewing the history and the time line of events ranging from the end of World War I to the end of World War II.

Teachers posting a time line of significant events should remind students that often the protagonists, Anne Frank, for one, were unaware of all that was happening.

A vocabulary list of the period, including terms such as *Gestapo, concentration camp,* or *anti-Semitism,* serves as a useful reference as well. A glossary of terms that can be ordered (at no cost) through the Simon Wiesenthal Center will facilitate the reading and alert students to euphemisms employed by the Third Reich such as "police actions" (round ups that typically meant mass murder), "resettlement" (deportation), and finally "Final Solution" (the planned annihilation of every Jew in Europe). These mild phrases corrupted the language and masked the evil intent. Through this study of language, teachers and students become aware that even the sounds of language, (*Kristallnacht,* for the Night of Broken Glass) are deceptive.

Journal writing is a key component to understanding the Holocaust and its literature. The journal becomes a vital link to feelings, an outlet for emotions, and an opportunity to begin to raise questions. The topic "Why should we learn about the Holocaust?" may be assigned early in the unit to evoke students' background knowledge, and understanding. Journal responses to this question, shared in a group, are useful in developing a rationale. As students read, write, reflect, and discuss, they should be cautioned against judging the actions of the victims. It is helpful for students and teachers to question how, in a world stripped of cultural norms and the support of its values, anyone can ever know what he or she would do in such a dire situation.

After a week or two of readings and discussions, the teacher may ask students to develop culminating projects. They may write essays, plays, poems, research papers, and create visual displays. One creative student tallied the number of victims and survivors per country by collecting kernels of rice, each one representing a thousand people. The skinny book idea, in which students create and edit their own abridged collection of works on a specific topic, also functions well for a unit on the Holocaust (Epstein, 1996, p. 496). As students are given the opportunity to share their readings and projects, they gain the perspectives of different genres and the insights of their peers.

To offer students a choice of readings and research projects respects and accommodates their interests and sensitivities. Some students are affected more by fiction than nonfiction; others will want to delve into details of a particular concentration camp. Teachers who provide a selection of genre—poetry, literature, and the media (videos such as *The Wave* and *One Survivor's Story* are excellent)—find this variety helps to maintain student interest. Technology is particularly responsive to individualized research, with CD-ROM disks on Anne Frank and a geographical atlas of the Holocaust, in addition to many Web sites. Anti-Defamation League publications are available to teachers and students who must be alert to hate Web sites, and the forms of Holocaust denial.

Guides for Teachers of Holocaust Literature

In their article, "Teaching about the Holocaust: Rationale, Content, Methodology, and Resources," Totten and Feinberg outline steps to developing clear rationales early in the unit (1995, p. 323). Strategies can also be found in the guidelines from the United States Holocaust Memorial Museum. Totten and Feinberg also suggest teachers should revisit students' responses to the question "Why learn about the Holocaust?" to maintain focus and signal to students that their readings are not simply another piece of historical fiction or nonfiction (p. 323). In addition, they provide a list of thought-provoking rationales generated by educators, among them, "To gain insight into why the Holocaust and thus, other genocidal acts are *not* inevitable" (p. 324).

Some guides suggest simulation activities to crystallize the experiences of prejudice and discrimination. However, these activities can never truly duplicate extreme situations of hunger and fear; and moreover, such exercises can be dangerous to young psyches. An activity such as "Loss of Identity" is a more useful tool to give a class clues about how insidiously a human being can be deprived of rights, freedoms, humanity, and eventually of life itself. In this two-day activity, students are first asked to write a journal entry identifying themselves for someone who does not know them. The class then shares and discusses what comprises an identity. Following this session, each student fills out an identity chart and supplies such factors as name, gender, hair color, language, family, friends, pets, favorite activities, places, clothes, and most important possessions. The second day, as students are seated in a circle, the teacher, acting as a fictitious dictator and reading from a script, requires the students to cross out factors one at a time until each student is left only with his or her age, language, and gender. The students are then asked to make a connection between their loss and the events that led to the Holocaust. More detailed information on the identity graph may be found through the Capital Area Writing Project.

Holocaust literature is at once engaging. Books such as *The Devil's Arithmetic* and *Gentlehands* strongly attest to the literary value of young adult literature itself. To make meaning of a book such as *Night* is to go through a process of changing relationships toward the text, as conceived by Judith Langer (1990, p. 813). Although these processes occur and recur throughout the reading, some Holocaust literature particularly distills the experience of each perspective.

> Being Out and Stepping In: Students make initial contact with the reading. In *Night*, it is immediately terrifying.
>
> Being In and Moving Through: Students become immersed in the reading, which may be accomplished in bits or for an extended period of time. In *Anne Frank: The Diary of a Young Girl*, this becomes an inner journey.
>
> Being In and Stepping Out: Students personalize the reading. In *The Devil's Arithmetic*, this becomes a sense of appreciation for Chaya.
>
> Stepping Out and Objectifying the Experience: Students are able to critically judge the content and experience of the reading from a distance. In *Gentlehands*, students question the grandfather-grandchild relationship.

Well phrased, thought-provoking questions unique to stories of rescue, resistance, memoirs, and so on, are contained in a wonderful guide to teaching the Holocaust, *Learning about the Holocaust: Literature and Other Resources for Young People*.

Perhaps the best guide to see a teacher through the unit is the concept of balance. Teachers need to seek a balance by respecting the students' right to know with their right to avoid horror, by providing readings of rescuers and by recognizing the uniqueness of the Holocaust, even as one relates to other instances of oppression in history.

As the unit comes to an end, teachers and students discover together that they are changed. As inspiring as the works of known authors are, so are the works of the students. Save them, put them up, and make sure they are read. We hope students will have emerged from this unit with the same conviction as Anne Frank, "in spite of everything, I still believe that people are really good at heart. I think that it will all come out right, that this cruelty too will end. . . . In the meantime, I must uphold my ideals, for perhaps the time will come when I shall be able to carry them out" (1953, p. 237).

Practical Guides and Resources

Anti-Defamation League, 823 United Nations Plaza, New York, New York 10017. E-mail: www.adl.org

Bachrach, S. D. (1994). *Tell them we remember: The story of the Holocaust.* Boston: Little, Brown.

Brown, J. E., Rubin, J. E., & Stephens, E. C. (1995). *Learning about the Holocaust: Literature and other resources for young people.* North Haven, CT: Library Professional Publications.

Danks, C. & Rabinsky, L. B., (Eds.) (1999). *Teaching for a Tolerant World, Grades 9–12.* Urbana, IL: NCTE.

Gibbs, L. J., & Earley, E. J. (1994). *Using children's literature to develop core values.* Bloomington, IN: Phi Delta Kappa Educational Foundation.

Simon Wiesenthal Center Library and Archives, 9760 W. Pico Blvd., Los Angeles, CA 90035-4792. Phone: (310) 553-9036. E-mail: library@wiesenthal.com

The Holocaust Library Book Series. 1997. San Diego: Lucent Books.

United States Holocaust Memorial Museum. *A resource book for educators: Teaching about the Holocaust.* Washington, DC: United States Holocaust Memorial Museum. Outreach Request Telephone Hotline: (202) 488-2661. E-mail: education@ushmm.org

Willis, Dr. Aaron. (1997). *Teaching Holocaust studies with the Internet: Internet lesson plans and classroom activities.* Lancaster, PA: Classroom Connect.

References

Allport, G. W. (1954). *The nature of prejudice.* Cambridge, MA: Addison-Wesley.

Bartel, R. (October 1983). Growth and regression through language. *English Journal, 72* (6), 44–46.

Mansilla, V. B., & Gardner, H. (January 1997). Of kinds of disciplines and kinds of understanding. *Phi Delta Kappan, 78* (5), 381–86.

Brown, J. E., Rubin, J. E., & Stephens, E. C. (1995). *Learning about the Holocaust: Literature and other Resources for young people.* North Haven, CT: Library Professional Publications.

Bunting, E. (1980). *Terrible things: An allegory of the Holocaust.* Philadelphia: The Jewish Publication Society.

Carnegie Council on Adolescent Development. (1990). *Turning points: Preparing American youth for the 21st century.* Washington, DC: The Council.

Drew, M. A. (February 1991). Merging history and literature in teaching about genocide. *Social Education, 55* (2):128–29.

Drew, M. A. (October 1995). Incorporating literature into a study of the Holocaust: Some advice, some cautions. *Social Education, 59* (6): 354–56.

Epstein, B. B. (March 1996). Creating skinny books helps students learn about difficult topics. *Journal of Adolescent and Adult Literacy, 39* (6): 496–97.

Farnham, J. F. (April 1983). Ethical ambiguity and the teaching of the Holocaust. *English Journal, 72* (4): 63–68.

Fisch, R. O. (1994). *Light from the yellow star: A lesson of love from the Holocaust.* University of Minnesota: Yellow Star Foundation.

Frank, A. (1953). *Anne Frank: The diary of a young girl.* New York: Pocket Books.

Gillespie, T. (December 1994). Why literature matters. *English Journal, 83* (8): 16–21.

Goldberg, M. (February 1995). Children's literature and the Holocaust. *Selected papers from the Annual Conference of the International Association of School Librarianship, Pittsburgh, Pennsylvania, July 17–22, 1994 (ED 399 955).*

Hennings, D. G. (February 1993). On knowing and reading history. *Journal of Reading, 36* (5): 362–70.

High-tech hate: Extremist use of the Internet. (1997). New York: Anti-Defamation League.

Holocaust denial: A pocket guide. (1997). New York: Anti-Defamation League.

Innocenti, R. (1996). *Rose Blanche.* San Diego: Harcourt Brace.

Kerr, M. E. (1978). *Gentlehands.* New York: Harper & Row.

Kohlberg, L. (June 1975). The cognitive-developmental approach to moral education. *Phi Delta Kappan, 56* (10): 670–78.

Langer, J. (December 1990). Understanding literature. *Language Arts, 67* (8): 812–16.

Lowry, L. (1989). *Number the stars.* Boston: Houghton Mifflin.

Mahle, B. (October 1985). The power of ambiguity: Elie Wiesel's *Night. English Journal, 74* (6): 83–84.

McGowan, T. M., Erickson, L., & Neufeld, J. A. (April/May 1996). With reason and rhetoric: Building the case for the literature-social studies connection. *Social Education, 60* (4): 203–6.

Reissman, R. (May 1995). In search of ordinary heroes. *Educational Leadership, 52* (8): 28–31.

Richter, H. P. 1987. *Friedrich.* New York: *Puffin Books.*

Rudman, M. K., & Rosenberg, S. P. (Summer 1991). Confronting history: Holocaust books for children. *The New Advocate, 4* (3): 163–76.

Schlene, V. J. (February 1991). Teaching about genocide. *Social Education, 55* (2): 82–83.

Sherman, G. W. and Ammon, B. D. (March 1998). Children's literature in cyberspace. *Book Links, 7* (4): 58–63.

The capital area writing project. Box 7801, 402 Poe Hall, School of Education, North Carolina State University, Raleigh, North Carolina 27695-7801. Phone: (919) 515-1784. E-mail: ruie@poe.coe.ncsu.edu

Totten, S., & Feinberg, S. (October 1995). Teaching about the Holocaust: Rationale, content, methodology, and resources. *Social Education, 59* (6): 323–33.

Volavkova, H. (Ed.). (1993). *I never saw another butterfly: Children's drawings and poems from Terezin concentration camp, 1942–1944.* New York: Schocken Books.

Willis, Dr. A. (1997). *Teaching Holocaust studies with the Internet: Internet lesson plans and classroom activities.* Lancaster, PA: Classroom Connect.

Yolen, Jane. (1990). *The devil's arithmetic.* New York: Puffin Books.

Zack, V. (January 1991). "It was the worst of times": Learning about the Holocaust through literature. *Language Arts, 68* (1): 42–48.

Marlene B. Hartstein is instructor of reading at Montgomery College in Maryland and is a reading specialist for the Montgomery County Schools in Maryland. Hartstein attended the Holocaust Institute of the Board of Jewish Education, Washington, DC, and Harvard Graduate School of Education Writing, Reading, and Civic Education Institute. She has conducted independent research in Holocaust literature, altruistic behavior, and civic education. She has presented at many state and local conferences, including NCTE and the IRA World Conference on Reading. Hartstein has been awarded grants by the Washington Post and the Maryland Middle School Association.

Karen Zelde Schejtman Sultan teaches English and reading at Takoma Park Middle School in Montgomery County, Maryland. She wrote the Montgomery County seventh-grade English curriculum for teaching the Holocaust. Sultan has an undergraduate degree from Rutgers University and a Masters degree from Virginia Commonwealth University. She has presented at state and national conferences including NCTE and IRA.

6 Telling Lewis Hine's Story: Russell Freedman's *Kids at Work*

Myra Zarnowski
Queens College, Flushing, New York

In the years before World War I, this country witnessed and tolerated a condition referred to as "industrial slavery" (Wormser, 1996). Two million children under the age of sixteen worked in factories, mills, mines, and canneries—some as young as four years old. They worked for twelve hours or more, for outrageously low wages, doing work that was dangerous, dreary, and dull. Unlike the apprenticeship work of previous generations, this work did not prepare them for a better, more prosperous life; instead, it prepared them for more of the same. As industries expanded, factory owners needed an ever-larger supply of cheap labor. They rationalized that by employing children they were providing them with safe, purposeful work. After all, in some cases, weren't they working right alongside their parents?

The true stories of child labor at the turn of the century, while quite vivid and disturbing, are remote from the everyday experiences of most of the children we teach. They don't work in mines, factories, or canneries; they don't work twelve to sixteen hour days; and they don't work at dangerous jobs under hazardous conditions. The challenge, then, for authors such as Russell Freedman, is to help children connect with this experience. As they learn about the lives of children who lived almost one hundred years ago, they broaden their concept of childhood—what it has been and what it is, and what it could be.

In *Kids at Work*, Russell Freedman explores the world of child labor during the years 1908–1918, when Lewis Hine worked as an investigative photographer for the National Child Labor Committee (NCLC). Hine's writing and the photos that he gathered from across the country revealed a "shocking reality that most Americans had never seen before" (Freedman, 1994a, p. 5). It is Russell Freedman's skillful intertwining of three distinct sources of information—facts, photographs, and the focused experience of a single individual (in this case the social reformer Lewis Hine)—that provides readers with the basis for *compassionate imagining*, a blending of both knowing and caring about the past. A closer look at these sources will show that they are not only additive but that they contribute to the cumulative impact of the book.

Facts

Developing *compassionate imagining* requires access to the facts. What happened? To whom? When? Why? How? Until recently, reading for the facts, or taking the efferent stance, has been regarded as passive and detached. The process of accumulating information has been associated with memorization and regurgitation of information. It has been termed uninspiring and coldly cognitive.

This is no longer the case. We are beginning to understand that information seeking can be a truly motivational experience that not only satisfies our curiosity but also leads to greater personal understanding. Exploring factual material enables readers to "find themselves" in the content rather than "lose themselves" in the story (Alexander, 1997, p. 86). Historical narratives, in particular, provide the background for situating ourselves in the flow of history. They satisfy children's "need to know" (Levstik, 1986, p. 9) about truly dramatic and complex events that still reverberate with our experiences today.

A new perspective on reading—one that moves beyond the dichotomy of either efferent or aesthetic reading, or even a combination of both—means that we also need to encourage responses to social issues emerging from the world beyond the individual (Allen, 1997; Creighton, 1997; Yenika-Agbaw, 1997; Zarnowski, 1995). To develop such a critical perspective, readers need the facts.

Russell Freedman understands that information can be motivating. Therefore, he assumes a storyteller's stance in order to write about history in a compelling way (1992, 1993, 1994a). According to Freedman, "I think of myself first of all as a storyteller, and I do my best to give dramatic shape to my subject, whatever it may be" (1994a, p. 138). From this stance comes his use of storytelling techniques, namely the use of vivid, detailed scenes; characters developed through the use of small but "telling" details; and use of personal anecdotes. He uses each of these techniques in *Kids at Work* (1994b). First, he opens the book with *vivid, detailed scenes*, as shown in the following description:

> Manuel is five years old but big for his age. When the whistle
> blows at 3 o'clock in the morning, he pulls on his clothes and

hurries to the shrimp and oyster cannery where he spends the day peeling the shells of iced shrimp. He has been working as a shrimp-picker since he was four. (p. 1)

Other descriptions include scenes inside a cotton mill:

The machinery made such a racket, workers had to shout to be heard above the din. And because heat and moisture helped keep the cotton threads from breaking, the mill windows were always kept closed. The hot, steamy air was filled with dust and lint that covered the workers' clothes and made it hard to breathe. (p. 35)

A glass factory is described as follows:

The temperature of molten glass is 3,133 degrees Fahrenheit. The temperature in the glass factories ranged between 100 and 130 degrees. Fumes and dust hung in the air. Broken glass littered the floors. It wasn't surprising that cuts and burns were the most common injuries. (p. 54)

Descriptions such as these help the reader envision the setting.

A second storytelling technique consists of revealing facts about characters through the use of *telling details*. We learn details about Lewis Hine who disguised his identity, "posing as a fire inspector, or an insurance salesman, or an industrial photographer who was after pictures of buildings and factory machinery" (Freedman, 1994b, p. 26). He "often resorted to tricks in order to get the pictures he wanted. . . . Hine knew the height of each button on his vest from the floor, so he could measure a child standing alongside him with no one being the wiser" (p. 29). These small but significant bits of information help us understand that for Hine gathering data was his most important concern, and that the ends—even when they included trickery—justified the means.

We learn that Hine related well to his young subjects, communicating a caring attitude. When asked why all his children appeared to be so beautiful, Hine replied, "I only photograph beautiful children" (Freedman, 1994b, p. 86). He seemed to have a reassuring manner that convinced children that he was on their side.

Finally, we learn that in his later years, Hine modestly recommended a much younger colleague and friend who was seeking employment as "a new and better Hine" (Freedman, 1944b, p. 86). He did this even though he himself was in desperate need of work. Through detailed glimpses such as this, full of *telling details,* readers develop insight into Hine's character.

A third storytelling technique consists of facts revealed through the use of *anecdote.* To show us the uncaring attitude of mill operators,

Freedman tells us about an incident reported by Hine. "'We don't have any accidents in this mill,' the overseer told [Hine]. 'Once in a while a finger is mashed or a foot, but it don't amount to anything'" (Freedman, 1994b, p. 35).

To show the terrible conditions in the glass houses, Freedman reports that workers refused to allow their children to work there. One worker told Hine, "I would rather send my boys straight to hell than send them by way of the glass house" (Freedman, 1994b, p. 57). Such anecdotes—short yet powerful—bring the facts of child labor to life.

Photographs

Readers of *Kids at Work* cannot fail to be moved by the numerous photographs taken by Lewis Hine. What is it about them that still remains so moving after all these years? Among the reasons critics offer for their powerful impact is Hine's use of the *direct eye*. Not only are most of the children shown in a straightforward, frontal position—often softened by light shining down on them—they also make eye contact with the observer. Using this *direct eye*, Hine showed viewers the conditions under which children worked in mills, canneries, mines, farms, and factories. He showed "people who walked to work at six in the evening when all families were supposed to be sitting down to dinner. It was the eye that told people what went on inside the areas of life they never experienced. But never softly. Never meekly" (Gutman, 1974, p. 46). As critics have pointed out, Hine showed middle-class viewers that despite the brutal conditions and terrible settings, "the children of the poor were not unlike their own" (Curtis & Mallach, 1984, p. 25).

In addition, these photos also show us the conflict between the aesthetic and the historic. The purity of the child, classically posed, contrasts with the unsuitable surroundings. The nobility of the human will clashes with the factory and the gate. Hine was completely aware of this. He purposefully joined his social convictions about the evils of child labor with his photographic purposes. "Photographically he learned that the image which packed the most powerful social punch was that with the strongest aesthetic impact, because this was the image that most effectively made the public a witness to the scenes of degradation that filled his angry vision these years" (Rosenblum & Trachtenberg, 1977, p. 128).

Then, too, there is the sheer volume of the photographs and the extensiveness of Hine's reporting. In *Kids at Work* there are photos on every other page. And while they are drawn from mills, farms, mines, factories, and streets, they all argue the same point: Child labor is wrong; child labor is evil. Even this convincing sample is but a small portion of the more than five thousand photographs that Hine took for NCLC as he traveled across the country, covering as much as fifty thousand miles a year. As one critic notes, "it was the mass and weight of Hine's evidence that was so convincing" (Goldberg, 1993, p. 175).

The Focused Experience of a Single Individual: Lewis Hine

Biography, the life of a single individual played out against the large backdrop of society, provides a third source of *compassionate imagining*. By studying the lives of individuals, children come to understand that one person can indeed make an impact for good or for evil.

In *Kids at Work* the story of child labor is told through the life of Lewis Hine, teacher-crusader. His life story is an extraordinary case of social efficacy. Freedman not only refers to Hine's work as a crusade, but he emphasizes that Hine was at heart a teacher. Braving danger, Hine set out to make changes—to enlighten. According to Freedman, "As Hine traveled, he discovered that investigating child labor was like entering an armed camp. Owners and managers regarded the little man with a big box camera as a troublemaker" (1944b, p. 24). Who would not root for this social reformer risking his safety to protect children, a perfectionist constantly worried that since he was resorting to tricks to gain his data, the data itself must remain 100 percent pure?

Hine was an educated reformer, who can also be thought of as a "sociologist-photographer." He had studied sociology at Columbia University and was clearly sympathetic to the progressive movement. His art served his social agenda. For Hine, the camera was an "instrument of truth. . . . He was absorbed by social results, not technical perfection" (Rosenblum et al., 1977, p. 119). In a chapter entitled "Making a Difference," Freedman tells us, "Hine's photos were meant to shock and anger those who saw them. They were intended to mobilize public opinion, and that is exactly what they did" (1994b, p. 72).

Finally, Hine was a spiritual crusader. Referring to his own work, Hine remarked that "the human spirit is the big thing after all." His dedication to moral principles is clear. According to his friend Walter Rosenblum,

> Hine regarded his work as a moral responsibility. . . .And the greatest of all crimes, the exploitation of children as laborers, would wither the hope and grace of the young. This degradation

was to become his obsession; it would give him no rest. No matter the weather or his state of health, Hine was in the field documenting the misery of exploited children." (Rosenblum et al., 1977, p. 12)

The career of Lewis Hine—teacher-crusader, sociologist-photographer, and spiritual crusader—connects readers to the past and provides entry into *compassionate imagining*.

From *Compassionate Imagining* to Contemporary Concern

When reading *Kids at Work*, readers can draw on the three sources to develop *compassionate imagining:* facts told in an interesting way from the perspective of a masterful storyteller; photographs that make a lasting impression because of the clash of the aesthetic and historical; and biographical information about a crusader against evil.

This book puts the spiritual, moral, and ethical concerns of ordinary children at the center of the conversation. Not politics or power; not weapons and warfare; not expansion or empires—*Kids at Work* focuses on the quality of the lives children lived as a result of industrialization in this country. It speaks to our basic concerns about health and well-being—what Nell Noddings (1992a, 1992b) refers to as an "ethic of caring," a focus on matters of spiritual concern. Noddings's challenge to structure the curriculum not around disciplines but around caring is consistent with Hine's insistence that "the spirit is the big thing after all."

As we read books dealing with social issues, books designed to promote *compassionate imagining,* we need to raise questions that support a curriculum of caring, one concerned with the human spirit. We need to ask questions such as the following: What does this book teach us about being more compassionate? What does it say about social change and how it comes about? What parallels does this story have for me and my life, and the lives of people I know? What about the lives of people I do not know?

Freedman helps bridge *compassionate imagining* with contemporary concern. He tells us that the crusade is not over. There is more work to be done. He reports:

> Compared to conditions in 1904, when the National Child Labor Committee was founded, gratifying progress has been made. Still, child labor has not vanished from America. It exists today among the children of recent immigrants who toil next to their mothers behind the closed doors of sweatshops; among a half-million poverty-wracked children of migrant farm workers; among hun-

dreds of thousands of youngsters who hold jobs prohibited by law, or who work excessive hours while attending school. (1994b, p. 97)

As Freedman ends the book, he reminds us that the (NCLC) is still working and that yearly awards are now being given in the name of Lewis Hine. This is a timely and significant reminder that *compassionate imagining,* while a noteworthy goal, is but the foundation for contemporary concern.

Sharing *Kids at Work* with Middle School Students

Because *Kids at Work* is such a rich combination of history and art, students can respond to it in a number of different ways.

Investigating the Elements of *Compassionate Imagining*

Draw attention to the three complementary sources of information in *Kids at Work*—facts, photos, and firsthand information. Students can use a web to focus their discussion of each source of information, adding the specific examples they identify. When discussing facts, make a list of the *vivid, detailed scenes, telling details,* and *anecdotes* that Russell Freedman provides in his writing. When discussing photos, list both the information they provide and the feelings they generate. When discussing the firsthand information (in this case, the biographical information about Lewis Hine), list the evidence that he was a teacher-crusader, sociologist-reformer, and spiritual crusader. When the Web is complete, students can discuss how the three sources of information work together to promote *compassionate imagining* (see Figure 6.1).

Spending a Day with Lewis Hine: Simulated Journal

Students can imagine that they were alive when Lewis Hine was taking his photographs for NCLC. Ask them to write about a day—or a series of days—they spent with him, visiting a factory, coal mine, or farm that employed children. What did they notice? What did they think about what they observed? Encourage students to think about and report on conversations they might have had with Hine during the time they spent together.

Examining the Language of Child Labor: Making a Word Wall

To describe the conditions under which children worked, Freedman uses many labor-related words in *Kids at Work*. Students can skim the text in order to list these words and sort them into groups that belong

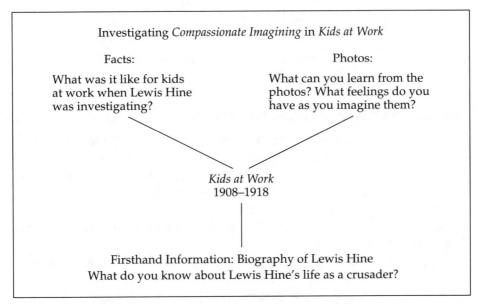

Figure 6.1. Web for Discussing *Compassionate Imagining*

together. A word wall can be used to gather these words together. While the experience of identifying and sorting these words is a valuable activity in itself, having the words visible in the classroom promotes their later use in other types of writing such as journals, essays, poetry, dialogues, and more. Some sample word groups that might be included in a word wall are listed in Table 6.1.

Writing Poems for Two Voices

In *Seeing Whole through Social Studies* (1995), Tarry Lindquist explains that writing poems for two voices is an excellent way to explore different perspectives on the same issue. Based on Paul Fleischman's book *Joyful Noise: Poems for Two Voices* (1992), which can be used as a model of this kind of writing, these poems are meant to be read by two people. Speakers should read the lines in order, from top to bottom. Some lines, they read together; others, they read separately. Their voices show the differing perspectives.

Using Russell Freedman's *Kids at Work*, students can develop one or more of the following contrasting perspectives:

The views of different child laborers (factory worker, mine worker, farm worker)

a factory overseer and a child laborer

two child laborers, past and present

Lewis Hine and a factory owner.

My example, which contrasts the views of a child laborer and a factory foreman, can easily be extended (see Figure 6.2).

The Writing Style of Russell Freedman

In an article entitled "Bring 'Em Back Alive" in *School Library Journal* (1994a), Russell Freedman discusses his style of writing history and biography. He uses storytelling techniques that include writing *vivid, detailed scenes*, small yet *telling details* about people, *quotations* that bring the person to life, and meaningful *anecdotes*. Students can look back through *Kids at Work* for examples of these features and make a chart displaying these examples.

To further investigate Freedman's style, look for examples of these stylistic features in other books by Russell Freedman such as *Lincoln: A Photobiography* (Clarion, 1987), *Eleanor Roosevelt: A Life of Discovery* (Clarion, 1993a) , *Franklin Delano Roosevelt* (Clarion, 1990), and *The Wright Brothers: How They Invented the Airplane* (Holiday House, 1991).

Researching Other Advocates for the Rights of Children

To complement the study of the life of Lewis Hine, students can research the life and times of other advocates or spokespersons for the rights of children. Leo Hart, who opened a school for "Okie" children during the Great Depression, is vividly portrayed in Jerry Stanley's *Children of the Dust Bowl* (Crown, 1992). Mother Jones, labor organizer, is brought to

Table 6.1. Words Used to Discuss Child Labor

Where Children Worked	Jobs Done by Children	Effects of Child Labor
canneries factories mines mills sweatshops farms city streets	spinner doffer sweeper oyster shucker mule driver coupler runner spragger gate tender newsie	respiratory diseases lack of education loss of childhood eye trouble heat exhaustion

Voice One: Child Laborer	Both Voices Together	Voice Two: Factory Foreman
	In a cotton mill	
the air is stifling with humidity and lint.		
		the air is humming with efficiency.
	Children tend machines, working as doffers, spinners and sweepers.	
We would rather be at school or play.		
		They are happy to be supporting their families.
	We're part of the expanding economy.	

Figure 6.2. An Example of Poems for Two

life in *Mother Jones: One Woman's Fight for Labor* (Clarion, 1995) by Betsy Harvey Kraft, and in Penny Coleman's *Mother Jones and the March of the Mill Children* (Millbrook, 1994). The work of Marian Wright Edelman, a contemporary spokesperson for children and president and founder of the Children's Defense Fund, is described in Beatrice Siegel's *Marian Wright Edelman: The Making of a Crusader* (Simon & Schuster, 1995). After reading one or more of these biographies, students can discuss the advocates' common concerns as well as the unique challenges they faced.

All of the activities begin and end with the appreciation of good nonfiction literature. Books such as *Kids at Work* open up socially relevant topics like child labor and help students understand our continuing need to question our goals and values.

References

Allen, A. M. A. (1997). Creating space for discussions about social justice and equity in the elementary classroom. *Language Arts, 74* (7), 518–24.

Alexander, P. (1997). Knowledge-seeking and self-schema: A case for motivational dimensions of exposition. *Educational Psychologist, 32* (2), 83–94.

Coleman, P. (1994). *Mother Jones and the march of the mill children.* Brookfield, CT: Millbrook Press.

Creighton, D.C. (1997). Critical literacy in the elementary classroom. *Language Arts, 74* (6), 438–45.

Curtis, V. P., & Mallach, S. (1984). *Photography and reform: Lewis Hine & the National Child Labor Committee*. Milwaukee: Milwaukee Art Museum.

Fleischman, P. (1988). *Joyful noise: Poems for two voices*. New York: HarperCollins.

Freedman, R. (1994a). Writing history and biography for young people. *School Library Journal, 40* (3), 138–41.

Freedman, R. (1993a). *Eleanor Roosevelt: A life of discovery*. New York: Clarion Books.

Freedman, R. (1990). *Franklin Delano Roosevelt*. New York: Clarion Books.

Freedman, R. (1994b). *Kids at work: Lewis Hine and the crusade against child labor*. New York: Clarion Books.

Freedman, R. (1987). *Lincoln: A photobiography*. New York: Clarion Books.

Freedman, R. (1991). *The Wright Brothers: How they invented the airplane*. New York: Holiday House.

Freedman, R. (1993b). "Bring 'em back alive." In M.O. Tunnell & R. Ammon (Eds.), *The story of ourselves: Teaching history through children's literature* (pp. 41–47). Portsmouth, NH: Heinemann.

Freedman, R. (1992). "Fact or fiction?" In E. B. Freeman & D. G. Person (Eds.), *Using nonfiction trade books in the elementary classroom: From ants to zeppelins*. Urbana, IL: National Council of Teachers of English.

Goldberg, V. (1991). *The power of photography: How photographs changed our lives*. New York: Abbeville Press.

Gutman, J. M. (1974). *Lewis W. Hine, 1874–1940: Two perspectives*. New York: Grossman.

Kraft, B. H. (1995). *Mother Jones: One woman's fight for labor*. New York: Clarion Books.

Levstik, L. (1986). The relationship between historical response and narrative in a sixth-grade classroom. *Theory and Research in Social Education, 14* (1), 1–19.

Lindquist, T. (1995). *Seeing the whole through social studies*. Portsmouth, NH: Heinemann.

Noddings, N. (1992a). *The challenge to care in schools: An alternative approach to education*. New York: Teachers College Press.

Noddings, N. (1992b). Social studies and feminism. *Theory and Research in Social Education, 20* (3), 230–41.

Rosenblum, W., & Trachtenberg, A. (1977). *America and Lewis Hine*. New York: Aperture.

Siegel, B. (1995). *Marian Wright Edelman: The making of a crusader*. New York: Simon & Schuster Books for Young Readers.

Stanley, J. (1992). *Children of the dust bowl: The true story of the school at Weedpatch Camp*. New York: Crown.

Wormser, R. (1996). *American childhoods: Three centuries of youth at risk*. New York: Walker.

Yenika-Agbaw,V. (1997). Taking children's literature seriously: Reading for pleasure and social change. *Language Arts, 74* (6), 446–53.

Zarnowski, M. (1995). Learning history with informational storybooks: A social studies educator's perspective. *The New Advocate, 8* (3), 183–96.

Myra Zarnowski is professor in the School of Education at Queens College, CUNY, where she teaches courses in language arts and children's literature. A former elementary and junior high school teacher, she now works with teachers to incorporate nonfiction literature into their language arts and social studies programs. She is the author of *Learning about Biographies: A Reading-and-Writing Approach for Children* and co-editor of *Children's Literature and Social Studies: Selecting and Using Notable Books in the Classroom*. She has contributed articles to the *Reading Teacher, English Record, Language Arts, Social Studies and the Young Learner* and the *New Advocate*. She is co-editor of the *New Advocate* column "Connecting Educators with Professional Materials."

7 Footprints in the Mud: Reading Science

Petey Young
Southern Oregon University, Ashland, Oregon

Some people can read footprints in the mud, "Here a coyote running quickly. Here a rabbit hops. There . . ." But many cannot. Some students can read science, but many cannot. Asking students to read science is often like asking them to read footprints in the mud. In each they know the ingredients: the alphabet, the words, the consistency of the mud, the forms in it. Meaning, however, is lacking.

This is, perhaps, the greatest insight reading research has given us: All literacy is context dependent. Within familiar spheres readers can follow the flow of a wide variety of material, even when it is unexpected. For example:

> Plant-visiting bats shatter the images held by people living in temperate zones. Instead of diving in silent pursuit of insects, these bats crawl clumsily through trees in noisy search of nectar or pollen. Their nocturnal habits are distinctive in that . . .

> Hearth tiles look dull after cleaning? Try dissolving two pieces of lump sugar in the juice of a lemon. Dip a soft cloth into this and rub the tiles all over. Dirt and stains will disappear and the tiles will dry with a shine that . . .

> Daniel bent close, half-blind with grief, his hands warm on her back. She wondered how much his sister had known. What her father would do next. "I love you too much to lose you," he sobbed. "You must promise me . . ."

Listeners at the NCTE meeting in Detroit followed these three leaps into unexpected subjects, yet appeared to have trouble with the following text:

> Our discussion involving time-symmetrical electrodynamics is based essentially upon the formula expressed by the absorber theory of radiation. If one thinks of the electromagnetic field associated with a particle we shall label '1', and if we sum over the fields of all particles except that of . . .

Although this text was shown on a transparency after it was read aloud, teachers acted confused, and, when given the classroom suggestion that it might help to read it slowly and carefully, some laughed.

Why is this fourth passage difficult? Most of us can pronounce each word in it, know what individual words mean, and even realize that the context must be physics or chemistry. Most reading researchers would tell us the difference lies in our ability to predict. But something more than this must be going on because many of us also lack experience or knowledge of bats or fireplace tiles, and many of us do not read romances and never will. Further, many of us were not particularly interested in hearing about bats, fireplace tiles, or Daniel's passion. But sometime in the past things have occurred in our lives that have made the first three familiar. What can we teachers do in the classroom to make the genre of science just as familiar to students?

Reading Science to Students

Educators hope that middle school students have been read to since preschool. Beyond a doubt, the genres that have been read to them with any frequency will have become the ones most familiar to their ears. Unfortunately, science has seldom been read to them and is therefore the least familiar. The genres most familiar to them are almost invariably those of adventure, mystery, biography, sports, comedy, fairy tales, and advertising. This has helped students in their ability to read, understand, and enjoy fiction (Routman, 1994), but, sadly enough, skill in reading fiction does not easily transfer to the genre of science. Science remains footprints in the mud.

By reading to students from science materials, classroom teachers can help the cadence of science become more familiar. Teachers can open science classes, as in this session, by reading a few paragraphs of interesting material based on the topic for the current lesson. To do this, the teacher gives no introduction to the material but simply begins to read as soon as it is time for science to begin. Reading lasts from three to five minutes and always stops in the middle of a sentence. The material read from is always left available in the classroom in case anyone wants to read it, but it is not discussed, explained, nor used as a required part of the day's activities.

To generate classroom discussion, teachers may read aloud to students other material from science; the opening reading, however, serves to serendipitously put the cadence of science in the air so that the tune of science can join the word-music already in students' heads. Sources of such material include introductions in science textbooks, chapters from science textbooks at various grade levels, newspaper articles, articles from *Science News*, biographies of scientists, and fiction involving science. Try it; it is an excellent technique for heightening interest in today's middle school students accustomed to the speed and interest of a quick-change TV culture (Young, 1991).

Finding the Characters, Plot, and Setting in Science

Students find the structure of science text is not the same as what has been familiar to them since they heard their first story. They learned long ago to follow how variations in characters, plot, and setting are presented in fiction. Now they need to apply this knowledge to science. Any unit in science can be interpreted in terms of the structure of fiction and doing so adds interest and clarity to the information in science texts (Young, 1992).

In science class, students read a piece typical of a science text, for example, a section on water erosion. Working in pairs or small groups, students then decide what elements could be the characters, what the setting is, and last what the plot is. Usually they start with a small section of text to prevent "the cast" from becoming overwhelmingly large or confusing. By focusing on a limited section of the text, the students process the information in terms they already know. They will come up with a variety of ideas: some quite imaginative, some mundane, all adding clarity to the text. In choosing who the characters would be were the passage on water erosion a story, the variety of responses range from the concrete—in which the characters become soil, water, and wind—to the abstract, in which the characters chosen are forces of nature such as gravity and planetary movement. Discussions follow and the reasoning behind the ideas turns minds on about the meaning. The settings the students choose tend to be similar but also vary from the concrete, the locality given in the text, to the abstract, such as planet earth. The plot is usually identical in each group; however, now the selection has an excitement that was lacking in the original text.

The way science is structured becomes friendlier when students examine its structure against the more familiar structure of fiction. Try it and see if your students show improved understanding of and enthusiasm for a science unit. Teachers at the NCTE meeting in Detroit tried this technique in groups of three. They applied the techniques used in fiction to paragraphs about moving water and the water cycle and found the exercise to be quick, fun, and interesting. Once a group struggles with the problem of imagining what the characters, plot, and setting of a nonfiction piece might be and then hears a variety of ideas from others, depth and richness are added to the information in the paragraphs. Adding fantasy is known to stimulate middle school readers (Wide, 1998).

Socializing with Science

Socializing in science is done through conversation circles, an activity that permits students to be social and gain deeper knowledge of science material at the same time.

The class is divided into three heterogeneous circles. Each circle receives two sets of 2-by-4-inch word cards. Because one in every five male students is to some degree color-blind and because insensitivity to yellow and blue is extremely rare, one set is yellow and one blue. Yellow signals students to create questions; blue, to create answers. The words on each set are identical; and on each set some bear asterisks indicating degrees of difficulty (see Figure 7.1). The cards can be used with any science unit and so are used over and over.

The activity is essentially student-directed, with the teacher moving from circle to circle. First, each student within a circle chooses two cards (one of each color and each having different words). Students then pair up by finding someone else in the circle who has one card with matching words. Next, the partners begin designing questions to fit the words on the yellow cards and answers that might fit questions asked by others from the words on the blue cards. Some word cards may not seem appropriate to the students, but that's fine: such words invite imaginative thinking, not unlike what readers do more easily with fiction. However cards in each set will outnumber the pairs of students in each circle so that a pair may exchange a card if they are convinced it "doesn't work" or "isn't any good."

Conversation begins when each pair has at least one question and one answer prepared. Questions are then presented clockwise around

WHICH IS . . .	WHERE IS. . .	WHAT IS . . .	HOW IS . . .
*HOW DOES. . .	*WHAT COULD . . .	*WHERE DOES. . .	*WHY DOES . . .
**WHEN MIGHT . . .	** WHAT IF . . .	**HOW COULD . . .	

Figure 7.1. Words Adapted from the Wiederhold Q-Matrix (1991)

the circle and are answered conversationally in no particular order, letting students practice the social skills of self-restraint and speaking up. The breadth and depth of possible questions that can be asked over material becomes clear to students as they discover that their prepared "answers" seldom fit the actual questions thought of by those who had the matching question cards.

After all its questions have been asked and answered, each circle chooses two of their questions to be carried by the authors to another circle. Each circle now gains four new people and loses four of its original members to another circle. The new pairs present their questions, and these, in turn, are answered conversationally within the new circle. The pairs then go on to the third circle so that everyone can hear and try to answer their questions. Thinking is stimulated not only by the variety students see generated by the same words but also from the wit and silliness of some questions and answers. We all know middle school students find such wit extremely memorable, and here is a cognitive activity that takes advantage of it.

Conclusion

Reading science appears to become more meaningful and exciting to middle school readers when teachers have students (1) hear science aloud so that the genre becomes familiar; (2) relate science to fiction by examining it in terms of plot, characters, and setting; and (3) share information socially in ways in which they retain control and use imagination. Otherwise reading science can often be too much like trying to read footprints in the mud because students (1) are unfamiliar with the cadence of science, having heard it less than the language of fairy tales, adventures, romances, murder mysteries, comedy, sports, and advertisements; (2) have not realized that science too has characters, plot, and setting; and (3) have not socially explored the meaning in exciting, successful ways with their peers.

References

Routman, R. (1991). *Invitations: Changing as teachers & learners.* Portsmouth, NH: Heinemann.

Wiederhold, C. (1991). *Cooperative learning and higher-level thinking skills: The Question Matrix.* San Juan Capistrano, CA: Kagan Cooperative Learning.

Wilde, J. (1998). Learning from fantasy. *Voices from the Middle, 5* (2), 40–42.

Young, P. (1991). Amazing what can happen when you read to them. *Journal of Reading, 35* (2), 148–49.

Young, P. (1992). Reader-friendly science. *Science Scope, 16* (1), 22–24.

Petey Young is professor of education at Southern Oregon University. She received her Ph.D. from the University of Wisconsin, Madison. Her specialty is reading comprehension. She has published articles with emphasis on reading in the middle grades in *Science Teacher, Scope, Reading Teacher,* and the *Journal of Reading.* She has taught in universities in Ghana, Malaysia, and Ethiopia; been a Fulbright scholar in Hungary; given workshops in Romania, Russia, and Brazil; lectured in the People's Republic of China, Belgium, and Japan; and presented a paper at UNESCO in 1992. Young has been affiliated with NCTE and IRA since 1980 and considers herself, first and foremost, a teacher.

II Reflective Practice in the Middle

How can I find time to reflect on my teaching practice?
How can I help my students reflect on their learning?
What can I do to help struggling students?
How can I know my students better?

Time to reflect on classroom learning and practice is a luxury for many middle level teachers. The writers in this section deal with the issues of reflective practice and thoughtful learning in different ways.

Cathy Fleischer teaches a graduate course that requires teachers first to reflect on their own literacy and then to reflect on the literacy of their students. The use of literacy portfolios as Cathy describes them in her piece has powerful potential for classroom teachers. Two of Cathy Fleischer's former graduate students share their experiences using portfolios as part of their practice. Jennifer Hannick Walsh discusses the ways in which her student literacy studies affected one of her students and how the development of his portfolio improved her teaching. Julie King reviews the results of one of her studies and explains how the study helped her to work with the student's parents so that the student could be more successful. This project continues to bear fruit years after its inception.

Rebecca Sipes shares how her work with one student caused her to reconsider the need for spelling instruction. Driven by the desire to help a struggling student, she studied ways for him to improve his spelling and become more confident about his writing. She shares what she has learned from this experience.

Janet Angelillo and Anna Reduce look at ways students can use a writer's notebook to help them become more reflective about their learning. They argue that students need to do more than record responses in a journal or log. The notebook provides a place for reflective thinking, and a source to which the writer returns again and again for material.

The essays in this section suggest ways to make reflection a regular part of the classroom experience for both teachers and students. Teachers should find ideas that will help them know and understand themselves and their students as readers, writers, and thinkers.

8 Sweating the Small Stuff: When Spelling Is More Than Small Stuff

Rebecca Bowers Sipe
Eastern Michigan University, Ypsilanti, Michigan

I *spotted the handwritten letter from his girlfriend lying casually on his desk. "Carter," I asked, "have you written her back?" With a steadfast look he replied, "I don't write."*

I was fortunate to be a writing project fellow in 1976, an event that literally changed my life as a teacher. I emerged from that experience with a new understanding of my own process as a writer and a keen commitment to helping adolescents deal with the "message" first and the "small stuff" later—as a part of their editing process. For a decade I reminded students that spelling was one of those features that could afford to wait until it was time to "clean up" the "sloppy copy" in order to create the "best draft." Carter helped me see things in a slightly different light. Though I continued to see spelling as a small part of the overall writing process, I came to understand that spelling problems were overwhelming Carter's ability to produce text. Watching him struggle—seeing him deny himself writing experiences that he might have otherwise enjoyed—ignited an interest in me to learn more about the dilemmas faced by poor spellers and the strategies that have proved helpful to them. I began to search for ways to support students like Carter: What could I, as a classroom teacher, offer such students to help them improve in spelling while I continued to support them as writers? This question became the focus of an ongoing study that continues to this writing.

Background

For Carter, spelling is more than just "small stuff." It is a major obstacle that confronts him every time he sits down to write. While most adept spellers can visualize words, such tools are generally unavailable or useless to Carter. At fourteen, he adheres rigidly to phonetic principles.

Sometimes, he reverses letters, and occasionally he mirrors whole words—or parts of words. It is not that his thinking is unclear. On the contrary, his written compositions, when he is willing to risk putting words on paper, are coherent and often thoughtful. In first-draft writing, few readers ever get beyond the chaotic spelling. With a certainty, writing completed under pressure and without adequate tools is a set up for Carter. In such cases, it is not uncommon for him to misspell every third word. Unfortunately, over the years classmates and teachers have tended to generalize from this dismal performance that since Carter cannot spell, he cannot write as well as others . . . he isn't as smart as others . . . he isn't as dedicated or as motivated as others . . . he is lazy about his work. Worse still, Carter has unconsciously bought into these generalizations as well.

It is important to note that Carter is not alone. According to one estimate, between 15 and 20 percent of all Americans have substantial difficulty with routine spelling, earning us the title of a nation of "closet poor spellers" (Kelly, 1992). What is more, our society levies stiff penalties against those who cannot spell. Contrary to Benjamin Franklin's suggestion that "an educated man should be able to spell any word at least six ways," we are a nation obsessed with spelling. Businesses judge prospective employees by misspellings on applications. Schools judge students based on writing done under test conditions. Peers are apt to tease and ridicule when routine words are misspelled. In the "real world" high expectations for correctness is a way of life.

While expectations for correct spelling are uniform, the playing field is clearly not level. Few allowances are made for individual differences. I've come to believe that students like Carter deserve strategies to help level the playing field.

Through interviews, focus groups, and in-service sessions, I have asked teachers to relate their own spelling histories. Most had little to tell: spelling was never a problem for them, so there was little of significance to remember. Some remembered lists of words, pre-tests and post-tests, and sometimes exercises during the week. No big deal. Others, however, recalled a bit more of a struggle. It took more effort to do well on the test on Friday, and sometimes the words "did not stick" in memory long enough to be useful in writing. Then there were the 20 percent who became very quiet, who told halting stories of feeling inadequate or stupid, of biting nails till they bled, of getting sick on Fridays to avoid spelling tests. Instinctively, I knew these were the folks who could help me make a difference for Carter. Somehow they had developed strategies that helped them navigate the spelling requirements of school and work despite their difficulties. I wanted to learn from them so that I could, in turn, share their secrets with students like Carter.

There is an assumption in the popular press that schools are no longer teaching spelling. In point of fact, the literacy histories that I collected indicate that—for poor spellers—schools never actually taught spelling. Instead, school was a place where lists of words were given and tested. Parents reviewed the words at home. Exercises, pre- and post-tests using a test-study-test methodology, and assignments to write words multiple times were all visual strategies that passed for instruction in school. For students with good visual memory, handing out lists was generally enough. Not so, however, for poor spellers.

One of the most apparent findings from the literacy histories collected thus far is that traditional spelling instruction (defined as receiving lists of words from a text or teacher, doing worksheet-type exercises, and taking pre- and post-tests) is not an effective method of instruction for poor spellers. In fact, weekly spelling tests tend to have countereffects in that they reinforce the student's lack of competence on a regular basis. Fortunately, other strategies have emerged that may provide the support needed.

In my work, I've identified three large categories that appear to be significant for spelling instruction: high-use words from one's own writing and from lists of high-frequency words; spelling rules and patterns; and spelling strategies.

High-Use Words

Poor spellers can learn much by examining their own first-draft writing. Errors typically are not made at random. We all have areas that cause us trouble. For me, it is word endings and silent letters within words. For others, the difficulty may lie elsewhere. The point is this: by systematically engaging students in error analysis and discussing the types of errors they make, the teacher helps students become better equipped to find those errors themselves. Taking this strategy one step further by recording "trouble-words" into a personal dictionary gives the student an ongoing tool for writing.

In my study, adults lamented time after time over the types of words they were required to study in school. "If I could have just concentrated on words that are used frequently, I would have been so much better off." How true. It comes as a surprise to many poor spellers to learn that as few as one thousand words make up about 90 percent of the words used in routine written communication. These are the words we see everywhere—and the lack of ability to spell them with some level of automaticity makes writing far more laborious than it need be. Actually, entire programs are available that focus on high-frequency words. Though I do not follow any of these as a rigid instructional tool, I have found these resources to be helpful. The point of all this to me is simply this: if these words are used so often and are, hence, so essential to routine communication, shouldn't they be stressed in the classroom?

I have introduced high-frequency lists to middle and high school students, laminated lists for their desks, put lists on the wall, and asked students to list in their own personal dictionaries words that really trip them up. We look for these words in magazines and newspapers and talk about particularly confusing pairs, for example, where/were, whether/weather, bother/brother. The more often students talk about the words, observe the words, and write the words correctly, the closer to automaticity they will get.

Spelling Rules and Patterns

Poor spellers often exhibit a surprising lack of awareness of patterns that exist in language. Students can better understand the reasons for so many variations in spelling rules if they know some history of our language. Students also find it interesting to learn that in Shakespeare's time, English was a language of about 50,000 words. Today the language has approximately 616,500 words and continues to grow at a rate of about 5,000 words a year. Where do all those "other" words come from? About 100 different languages have contributed to the English we know today. Obviously, with words coming into the language from so many different places, increased drill and practice on phonics will help us with some words but certainly not all words in the language (Gentry, 1981). For students who have substantial difficulty with spelling we must be sure they have all the tools they need. Any rule that holds true 70 percent of the time may prove valuable to a poor speller. Rules such as *"i before e except after c"* fit into this category. *Writers Inc*, one of the most frequently used handbooks on the market for secondary students, lists only four rules as well as the common exceptions to those rules. As with high-use words, attending to these rules may prove to be exceptionally valuable to poor spellers. In the same way that I advocate posting the high-frequency words, I favor putting these rules on the wall so they are in clear view all the time.

Patterns and word families are also important tools. As I worked with Carter, I came to realize that he believed the language to be totally random. He did not sense patterns of letter use and he had not spent time looking at how many words could grow from a single word base. As we webbed words that grew from the base of words such as "construct," he began to see the relationships that exist within the language. Helping students explore word study in this manner and covering the walls with the webs they create, helps poor spellers understand that patterns and word families do exist and can be extremely helpful in understanding the how (and why) behind spelling.

Spelling Strategies

For decades, I think I looked up the word accommodate every time I used it—until someone told me that I needed to accommodate the twins. That's all it took. The use of mnemonic devises often helps students remember the spelling of high-use words that may otherwise be tricky. Learning to use resources that list words broken into syllables but without definitions, spell checks, and dictionaries are essential for poor spellers. Some students must make use of tactile or musical strategies to hold on to correct spellings. With Carter we found tracing the "feel" of a word with a finger into the palm of his hand was an enormous help. Others identify words with music.

Most professional writers have editors. This is also a strategy. It's very important for struggling writers to know that even professionals may have difficulties with spelling. Poor spellers need to learn to look for trouble spots and to ask for editing help in final drafts. They also need to know that sometimes—depending on purpose and audience—spelling may be more important than at other times. I incorporated the use of editors through writing workshop. We all have strengths, and by encouraging students to collaborate and support one another, we all become both teachers and learners.

Final Thoughts

Support for poor spellers can be addressed in many ways. Mini-lessons taught as a part of writing workshop, individual instruction, or small group workshops provide opportunities for targeting instruction. For Carter, and the thousands of students like him, instruction in word study may be an essential element in creating a supportive writing environment.

References

Gentry, J. R. (January 1981). Learning to spell developmentally. *The Reading Teacher*, 378–81.

Kelly,   T. F. (April 1992). Spelling: Tyranny of the irrelevant. *Phi Delta Kappan*, 73 (8).

Sebranek, P., Meyer, V., & Kemper, D. (1996). *Writers inc: A student handbook for writing and learning*. Lexington, MA: Write Source.

Rebecca Bowers Sipe is assistant professor of English education and a co-director of the Writing Project at Eastern Michigan University. A twenty-five-year veteran of public school teaching and administration in Alaska, she has worked extensively in curriculum development and teacher education. Since joining the faculty at EMU, she has sought to draw methods students closer to public school classrooms through engagement with case study research, shared literacy histories, and collaborative literature reflections. Currently, she is working with middle school teachers to continue research aimed at identifying strategies that can be incorporated into classroom instruction to support these individuals.

9 Literacy Narratives

Cathy Fleischer
Eastern Michigan University, Ypsilanti, Michigan

I teach a course at Eastern Michigan University entitled "Literacy and Written Literacy Instruction," a course that might more aptly be titled, "What is this thing called literacy, anyway?" One of my goals in this course is to get students to question their own understandings of the term *literacy*. I am quite serious about this goal, and I even tell them on the first day that one of the measures of their success will be if they are less sure about the meaning of literacy at the end of the course than they are on the first day. Because literacy is a term whose meaning seems to vary depending on the historical moment, the social circumstances surrounding the occasion, the intent of the speaker of that term, and a thousand other variables, it's a term that almost defies understanding. When I hear the man in front of me in the grocery line complain about all the illiterates graduating from high school these days, what am I to make of his definition of literacy? When I hear a college professor rant about the illiterate essays written by the graduate students in his Shakespeare class, am I to assume he means the same thing? What about the book reviewer who raves about the literate voice of an author? Or the person quoted in the newspaper who complains that those who speak Black English just sound plain illiterate?

Alternately complicating and clarifying, these everyday versions of literacy are the abundant definitions posed by literacy scholars. E. D. Hirsch (1987) speaks of cultural literacy, a version of literacy that implies a shared cultural heritage. James Boyd White (1985) envisions instead a socially constructed literacy. J. Paul Gee (1986) speaks of an "essay-text literacy," a form-based literacy created for and maintained by schools. Resnick and Resnick (1977) talk about the history of literacy and a time in which literacy meant the ability to sign one's name. So, when teachers speak of literacy, do we mean any of these? Or do we mean the ability to score 50 percent on a statewide reading assessment? or the ability to read and interpret Shakespeare? or Toni Morrison? or Barbara Cartland? Do do we mean the ability to listen to a political debate on a voucher system for public schools and write a letter to the editor to express our beliefs?

Listening to both literacy scholars and everyday folks helps us understand that what is meant by literacy varies over time and place and that what we think of as a relatively stable term is, in truth, constantly changing, dependent in part on the social circumstances of a particular historic moment. What I want students to reflect on in this course is what they make of all these definitions, how the various understandings fit in with their own beliefs about literacy, what the implications are for those beliefs on their own teaching. In other words, the concept of literacy is problematic; literacy is always a representation of something, a naming of an individual or group of individuals that reflects as much about the namer's beliefs and values as it does about the person being named. How we as teachers situate ourselves in the representation intimately affects what we teach and how we teach.

Personal Literacy

I begin this journey with students by asking them to write about what they think literacy means. For some students this seems like the most mundane task in the world. "Literacy is a person's ability to read and write," they tell me. "A literate person is someone who can read and write enough to survive in the world." Or, according to a student last term,

> Literacy might be described as the ability of an individual to speak, read, and write in such ways as to demonstrate an understanding of language and the way it is used. Therefore, the lack of such ability, particularly in the written sense, would conclude that the previously mentioned individual could be considered illiterate.

Some students struggle with this question, thinking they were certain about the meaning of literacy until they actually tried to write it down. What does it mean to read and write enough to survive? What is enough? What about my dad who by society's standards is illiterate but who has survived very well for sixty-five years? For these students, literacy has been one of those terms that carries a nebulous meaning. They can use it in conversation with someone, they can insert it into an academic essay, but when asked to define it, they feel much less confident about their understanding of it.

One of my aims in the course is to help students question their own understanding of the term *literacy*, of their own practices as teachers of literacy, and to, as Knoblauch and Brannon say, "ask the explosively simple question, 'Why do it this way'" (1993, p. 11)? I want them to see that literacy is never a neutral term. As literacy workers in the schools, their stance toward literacy implies a whole set of beliefs that has everything to do with how they interpret the world around them: what they believe constitutes knowledge, what they believe about how people learn to read and write, what understandings and even values they hold about their own education, and how they believe others should be educated. I want them to see that the stance they hold toward literacy underlies their classroom practice. A lesson or exercise in class is never an isolated occurrence, but rather is situated within a whole belief structure.

Students read and write and think about what literacy has meant in their lives, what it has meant in others' lives, and what, imaginatively conceived, it could mean for everyone. And this is where literacy narratives come in. We begin by immersing ourselves in stories: the published accounts of others' literacy histories as well as the anecdotes and incidents of our own lives that seemed to have affected our personal literacy. We read the accounts of Linda Brodkey, Mike Rose, Victor Villenueva, and Min-zhan Lu and talk about their stories. At the same time, students join me in writing a series of short experiments. We recall our use of language from preschool through graduate school; remember occasions of reading and writing at home and how those differed from school experiences; explain our purposes for reading and writing at various points in our lives; discuss a time when we felt illiterate and try to figure out why we felt this way. Thinking about these experiences and comparing them to the experiences of Brodkey, Rose, Villenueva, Lu, as well as to the experiences of each other, helps students to uncover some significant "literacy moments," in their lives. Students then write a literacy memoir in which they analyze a few of those moments, trying to find connections among them in order to see how those moments have come together to constitute them as the persons they are, literate in particular ways. These papers always turn out to be revelations to the students. They are sometimes quite funny and often amazingly dramatic. Students recall teachers who opened the worlds of reading and writing to them; they recall the structures, such as libraries or houses, that served as the center of their literacy; they recall transitions—to new schools or new friends or new neighborhoods—as scary moments that sometimes helped and sometimes harmed their literacy. The unique statement of a person's literacy life always seems to help my students think not only about how their own stance about literacy was formulated but also how that stance might help them as teachers. Here are the words of two students who explained the significance of writing their literacy memoirs:

> Writing my literacy autobiography has helped me to see the truth about myself; how I strive to please others, how I need literacy in order to feel respected, and how my love of literacy brings me joy. I have learned how my parents and teachers have played such a dynamic role in creating my literacy, and how I, as a parent and a teacher, will affect the literacy of my children and my students.

And the second:

> In writing the autobiographical paper I was able to articulate some of the specific events that contributed to my sense of voicelessness. I wanted to conform in school and "be good" as my father expected at home. The things I wanted to talk or write about were not on the agenda at school or home. . . . I'm considering [now] the possibility that the complacency I've noticed in some students may be related to a similar difficulty in finding their voices.

Sometimes when teachers finish their narratives, they realize that many of the incidents that form the center of their stories run counter to what they do in their classrooms. They realize, for example, that as students they hated reading in school because it was prescribed, but they read voraciously at home where they had choice and time to pursue the pleasure of it. They recognize that in their own teaching, they have recreated their own schooling and thus have given students little choice. Other times, teachers recognize that their own experience has defined too narrowly their understanding of literacy and their pedagogy. They realize, for example, that because writing served as a means of discovery in their lives, they insist that all students write daily journal entries in which they reflect on their day-to-day existence. Once these teachers listen to the stories of their colleagues in our class whose experiences may have been quite different, they begin to reflect on this phenomenon: Do we too easily re-create our own literacy background into our teaching of all students?

Another's Literacy

This second response leads to the other major assignment of the course, in which I ask students to continue to step outside their own experiences to look at the literacy background of another person, someone whose literacy is quite different from their own. The charge to find someone whose background is unlike theirs is vital to help us recognize the depth of experiences people have with reading and writing and the different paths people travel on their journey toward literacy.

These pieces have been an education to me as well as to the students. I have learned about the literacy development of a plumber for whom books are an essential part of his life; a Romanian woman for whom books became an escape from the conflict surrounding her everyday life; a first grader who could talk quite easily about the themes of the latest book she had just read, *The Diary of Ann Frank;* the teenaged boy in an alternative school (for those kicked out of "regular school") who consistently walked out of class when asked to read or write; a teenaged girl for whom success in school depended on the depth of personal relationships she was able to forge with her female teachers . . . and on and on. When we talk about each other's papers and begin to immerse ourselves in the stories of so many others, our understanding of literacy is broadened far beyond what any scholarly text about literacy could do for us. As we read the stories of real people whose experiences are unbelievably varied, we participate in a "study of cases." We learn to be thoughtful about our own literacy experiences and to expand that understanding to the experiences of others. This expansion can change dramatically how we think about our teaching and how we connect with individual students and their parents.

Does any of this help my students get closer to an understanding of what we mean when we talk about literacy? I hope my students will leave with a more complex understanding of a term that is all too often used in very simplistic fashion and that they will see the many stories they have written, read, and heard as necessary and important complications, as they think about what literacy might mean for those they teach and those they know. As one of my students last term responded,

> Just as you promised, I cannot define literacy anymore than I could at the beginning of the semester. You messed it up for us just like you said you would. . . . If it's possible, you both confused me and opened my eyes at the same time. But I have a clearer understanding of things I had barely thought about previously on the subject. Somehow, I think that was the point anyway.

As far as I'm concerned, that's a success story.

References

Brodkey, L. (September 1994). Writing on the bias. *College English, 56* (5), 511–26.

Gee, J. P. (1989). Orality and literacy: From *the savage mind* to *ways with words. Journal of Education, 171* (1), 719–46.

Hirsch, E. D. (1987). *Cultural literacy.* Boston: Houghton Mifflin.

Knoblauch, C. H., & Brannon, L. (1993). *Critical teaching and the idea of literacy.* Portsmouth, NH: Boynton/Cook.

Lu, Min-zhan. (April 1987). From silence to words: Writing as struggle. *College English, 49* (4), 437–48.

Resnick, D. P., & Resnick, L. B. (1977). The nature of literacy: An historical exploration. *Harvard Educational Review, 47* (3), 370–85.

Rose, M. (1989). *Lives on the boundary.* New York: Penguin Books.

Villanueva, V. (1993). *Bootstraps.* Urbana, IL: National Council of Teachers of English.

White, J. B. (1985). *Heracles' bow: Essays on the rhetoric and poetics of law.* Madison: University of Wisconsin Press.

Cathy Fleischer, a former secondary English teacher, is currently associate professor of English at Eastern Michigan University and director of the Eastern Michigan Writing Project, a project that gives her multiple opportunities to learn with and from teachers at all grade levels. She is the author of *Composing Teacher Research: A Prosaic History,* co-editor (with David Schaafsma) of *Literacy and Democracy: Teacher Research and Composition Studies in Pursuit of Habitable Spaces,* and has authored a number of articles about literacy and teacher research. Her current research looks at teacher advocacy, connecting teacher research to community organizing strategies and theory.

Literacy Narratives: Knowing Students

Jennifer Hannick Walsh
Forsythe Middle School, Ann Arbor, Michigan

I began studying students using literacy narratives because I had a desire to understand those students who struggle with school. By studying many students over time, we can formulate a more complete view of different types of learners and the struggles they endure in attempting success. Likewise, we learn to constantly revise our definition of what literacy really is. It truly is different for children from different backgrounds and with different learning styles. It is essential that we write about the students we study. It benefits not only us, but the parents and other teachers in our buildings. Our special education teacher is now heard to say quite often: "You know how Jennifer chooses one student to study every year? Well, . . ." and then she goes on to talk of the impact of my study on a particular student's learning.

My Process

When selecting, I always try to choose a student who struggles. As someone who did not struggle in school, I am constantly trying to understand the difficulties many go through with their education. Also, I try to choose a student who is motivated to succeed. This shows me strategies a student may employ in order to be successful, and I may be able to use these strategies later to help others.

There is a process to gathering information, and usually it spans several months. Initially, students are surprised that I take an interest of this magnitude in what they are reading and writing. Additionally, explanation is necessary for the student as to why I feel this need to study them. Some students' initial reaction is that they have done something wrong or are behind in the class and want to know why the attention has been turned so intensely toward them. On the other hand, many students are flattered that such an interest is taken in what they do. I tell them I want to study how they learn so I can help them to be more successful, help their parents understand their learning process, and so that I will better understand how to help them with their difficulties.

I begin my study by interviewing students several times. The first is usually a get-to-know-you session. I ask students about family, school experiences, what is difficult for them, their interests, and where they see themselves in relationship to the rest of the class. This is a non-threatening way to get to know them and gather background information. Usually I ask questions that only a parent can answer, for example, *How did you learn to talk?* First, I have the student ask at home, and then I call or I set up an interview at school with the parent/s.

After several interviews have taken place, I collect data from the necessary files. Often there is a file I can access with test scores, MET results, specifics on learning disabilities, and goals for the school year. I also know what the school expects the student to be able to accomplish in any given quarter. This usually gives me valuable insight into the student's school history and what steps have previously been taken to ensure success. Additionally, I can compare test scores with what the student is actually able to accomplish in the classroom.

I feel it is important, as well, to consult existing research when I come across unfamiliar methods used to help the student in the past. For instance, when I worked with the student in my first study, her parents told me about all of the different methods her long-time tutor used to help her learn to read and decode meaning. Being unfamiliar with Orton Gillingham, I chose outside reading that dealt with a comparison between Orton Gillingham and whole language. This text helped me to see the benefits of both systems for students with learning disabilities.

By looking at the individual studies of students as small pieces in the puzzle of literacy, it is apparent after only studying a few how these pieces begin to fit together. Each of the students I have studied has had a different problem in school. By talking to students about the strategies they employ in making meaning, I gain insight into many different types of learning.

An Individual Study

I am working with a young man named Zack in my eighth-grade language arts class. Zack, a shy and introverted student with large childish writing, seldom speaks and struggles with school, especially writing. It is only since I have taken the time to study his literacy that I have discovered his other side and its relationship to his schooling.

Zack has a love of farming and spends every weekend with his father, helping to milk the cows, plant and harvest crops, and learn new techniques for agricultural efficiency. His knowledge is not school based, but farm based. Zack knows more about farms and farming than I could ever know. He uses critical thinking skills in relation to farming to improve crop and animal production. It is easy for Zack to articulate the exact procedure he and his father must follow in order to milk the cows, but he claims he has tremendous difficulty remembering dates and names for history tests.

Reports in Zack's file are incongruent with what I have observed about Zack in the classroom and through interviews. Although he reportedly reads at only a third-grade level, he can nevertheless read sophisticated farm reports and articulate the meaning and benefits of putting anhydrous ammonia in the soil. The term *Anhydrous ammonia* happened to show up in a story we were reading, and he returned later in the day to ask for its spelling and fill me in on its uses. His understanding of the farm, the equipment, and the crops and animals far surpasses what the average eighth grader knows about any profession. It was difficult for the school to see this literacy when he was constantly asked to write and read about things that were not as important to him as farming. Obviously, when reading about areas he understands, his potential far surpasses the third-grade level.

My interviews and classroom procedures have revolved around Zack's knowledge. I encourage him to write about what he knows, thus giving him more confidence with every piece he writes. Zack's papers are full of detail and knowledge of the farm. His latest piece, "Milking the Cows" shows, step by step, the process involved in his daily routine.

While I have worked to help Zack with mechanics and organization of his writing, the true knowledge for me comes from getting to know him as a person and how that benefits my ability to work with a student. I respect the farming knowledge Zack possesses, and I use that knowledge to further his writing abilities. We begin with writing about what he knows. He knows the stories he wants to tell, and I can ask honest questions about what I don't understand so he can add detail and clarify. The shy introvert is gone, replaced by someone who trusts me and the job I do. I've even seen some of his sense of humor emerge. He comes into my room to talk about what he is writing and to get information, something he never would have done in the past.

My study of Zack's literacy has benefited him as well. Zack is more than willing to work with me. He has learned that it is okay to be driven in one particular direction, and I see his confidence grow every day. He was the first one to tell me where his "tested" reading level was, but I pointed out that his specified knowledge moved far beyond anything a third or eighth grader could do. He left my room that day with a copy of James Herriot's *All Creatures Great and Small*. While intimidated by the size of that book, he was overjoyed when I explained that each chapter dealt with a new farm problem for the country veterinarian. Zack now sees how his knowledge can improve his life and the lives of others around him.

Zack is learning about his own literacy, identifying strengths and weaknesses, knowing where he has to go next. What we do in class gives legitimacy to his own stories and has released him from some of his introversion, so that his silence now has words.

Why do I continue to study the literacy of individual students? My initial study was for a graduate-school class, so why do I do it year after year? I realize that by getting to know an individual student, I gain insight into his or her learning and school experiences. As a form of professional development, literacy biographies help me revise my practice and evaluate the effectiveness of my teaching. Studying students' learning has helped me adjust curriculum more precisely to the needs of my students. With each student I study, I come to know myself better as a professional and as a learner.

Jennifer Hannick Walsh adores teaching language arts to eighth-grade students and has been teaching for ten years in the Ann Arbor Public Schools, Ann Arbor, Michigan. She holds a bachelor's degree from the University of Michigan and a Masters in Children's Literature from Eastern Michigan University. She has presented at MCTE on Teacher Narratives and their use in the classroom, and at NCTE on Literacy Biographies.

Literacy Narratives: Working with Parents

Julie A. King
Holmes Middle School, Lavonia, Michigan

I have traveled almost every conceivable route toward professional development: seminars, conferences, speakers, graduate-course work, partnering, mentoring, reading volumes of professional literature, and observing other teachers. Because I am by nature a lifelong learner, I constantly seek out opportunities to learn more about teaching literacy. I think one of the most important lessons I have learned in my first few years as a teacher is that I gain the most from accounts of actual teachers who learn from their own students. Teachers such as Nancie Atwell and Linda Rief first opened their classrooms to me, where I learned invaluable lessons from their students. My work with literacy biographies has further inspired me to listen to my own students and value my own instincts about what is happening in my classroom. Turning inward, I have become more and more a learner in my classroom, working with my students rather than above them. The most valuable professional growth I have gained through my teaching has been, by far, those lessons that only my students could have offered me.

While I do learn from all of my students in the dynamics of daily classroom life, I have found it valuable to take the time to do more specific studies with particular students. Because the pace of a middle school day can often blow to shreds time I might spend journaling, reflecting and writing about our classroom experiences, I find it important to set aside time to work with individual students to learn about them. As I recognize that my own literacy cannot dominate the whole of my teaching, I also realize that one student's experience is not necessarily indicative of all of my students. Nonetheless, the insight I gain from each individual student can go far in reminding me how personal any act of literacy can be. Often, I find strategies that are successful with one student may be worthwhile to try with others. More important, I learn over and over again how important it is to respect the needs of each of my students as I continually refine my teaching to meet the needs of all.

My first literacy biography was with Dean. When I received the assignment, my professor advised me to choose someone whose literacy background was different from mine. I immediately thought of Dean, a student in my eighth-grade language arts class. He had cerebral palsy and therefore had trouble communicating effectively with others, both verbally and in writing.

Working to learn about Dean's experiences had a huge impact on his parents. While I learned some things about his background through interviews with him, I needed to learn a lot by interviewing his mother. She related information about his elementary school experiences where reading and writing were great challenges for him. She spent numerous hours with her son, reading with him and discussing his work. During his eighth-grade year, however, he became far more private with her about his language arts experiences. In my classroom, he was excited about his writing, often offering to share with the entire class. In fact, one time, he actually conducted an entire class lesson around a piece he had written. As I talked with his mom, she described how he would come home from school and hide his writing folder, offering nothing to share with his family. I was so excited about some of his writing that I shared several pieces with her. Dean's love and appreciation of his family, as well as his great sense of humor were obvious in his writing. As she read his pieces, his mother began to cry, "I can't believe my Dean wrote this!" she exclaimed.

Because of my work with Dean and my communication with his parents, we discovered that writing was a medium through which he could develop and express his affective, emotional self in a way he was unable to do verbally. This was truly a breakthrough for Dean and his family. After reading the finished biography, they graciously sent me a letter of thanks. They wrote,

> In the end, we feel optimistic that despite Dean's handicap that the written medium can ultimately be his best method of language expression, provided he continues to train to improve his skills in this area. After reading your case study, we are determined more than ever to continue to encourage him to develop his written language skills to his absolute fullest potential.
>
> We want to thank you for taking such an intense interest in our son's development. Not only will it have helped you further your own educational and professional goals but it will also have helped our son immensely in an area where he is deficient but shows a lot of promise. In all of the years of professional care and attention that we have arranged for Dean, never has any one in-

dividual who has worked with him so accurately and insightfully captured the essence of his learning disability where language is concerned.

As Dean moved on to high school, his parents were committed to providing and encouraging writing experiences for their son. The things I learned from Dean and shared with his parents were incentive for them to continue to ensure that he had numerous opportunities to express himself in writing.

Julie A. King teaches language arts at Holmes Middle School in Lavonia, Michigan, where she also advises the school newspaper and ski club. In addition, she is a teacher co-director of the Eastern Michigan Writing Project. She is a graduate of Western Michigan University and holds a Masters degree in Written Communication from Eastern Michigan University. She is the co-author of "Becoming Proactive: The Quiet Revolution" in *Voices from the Middle*, March 1999.

10 The Writer's Notebook: A Place to Think

Janet Angelillo
Columbia University, New York, New York

Anna Danon Reduce
Columbia University, New York, New York

The writer's notebook is used as a tool in writing-process classrooms as a way to collect entries that build toward writing pieces. Teachers use the notebooks to guide students to the experience of a writer's life, that is, living with a conscious, reflective stance. However, the writer's notebook sometimes becomes a collection of meaningless or unrelated entries, and students do not go back to make meaning of their writing and thinking. When students receive a list of the kinds of entries they can write, they often go down the list, checking off each one as they write. A notebook like this is merely another assignment, a variation on teacher assigned compositions, and only appears to allow student choice.

While providing lists of possible notebook entries is valuable as a starting point, one way to elevate student work is to use the notebook as a place to develop and expand critical thinking skills. We have been studying three areas where the notebook could serve as a foundation for thought: a place for critical thinking, for research, and for making meaning within and across content areas. Our goal is to teach students that the notebook is to the writer what the canvas is to the artist and the instrument to the musician. We want students to see that the notebook is a workbench for writing and revising and also a place to discover and uncover thinking.

The Notebook as a Place for Critical Thinking

We have found that students who write to access their thinking often see themselves as thinkers and creators of ideas. The exploration of an idea in the notebook is a powerful experience. Students look back over entries to force connections or to discover the significance of their thinking and creatively expand original thoughts. Revisiting and rethinking an entry weeks or even months later is one way to help students develop ideas. They come to understand that original thinking and creative problem solving do not appear whole and complete the first time. Too often students believe the first idea or the first draft is enough to stand as completed work. We must lead them away from this fallacy.

Students need not only to strive for variety and depth in entries but also to see things from multiple perspectives, to elevate their observational skills, and to expand their own writing by using what others have written—both peers and published authors. Making sense of another's thinking is one way for adolescents to come to grips with their confusion about the world. Part of learning is grappling with issues and struggling to understand them. Thinking through their ideas by writing in a notebook is one way for students to develop an understanding of difficult or elusive concepts. Middle school students often have conflicting thoughts on the world, thoughts that anger or frighten them; the notebook is a place to work out this thinking.

We have words of caution here, however: while a notebook may be therapeutic, we are not practicing therapy. Be sure to refer any troubling entries to the proper school personnel. We tell our students that the notebook is public writing—if they write something, we will assume they want *us* to know about it, and, if necessary, *do* something about it.

The Notebook as a Research Tool

The writer's notebook is a vehicle for students researching a topic, as well as a means for researching themselves as readers and writers. Ideally, students carry their notebooks with them beyond the world of school, to the library, the park, the soccer field, the mall. They take field notes the way a scientist would, or might; they practice living *carefully*, as an artist, composer, or mathematician might. Seeing things from multiple perspectives helps students begin to see interconnectedness and develop habits of mind in various disciplines.

Middle school students often feel lost and alienated. It is empowering for them to live with a topic and learn to know something deeply, to become experts. An archeologist once said that he only recognized a human elbow bone among hundreds of scattered rocks because he had lived with human bones for so long. Our students need to live with something and to know it that deeply. The thing they know so well may not be an academic topic; we have seen eighth-grade boys get excited about researching dirt bikes and rock music. The important thing is commitment to the topic and being aware of it all day long, living with it through the day. Whatever the topic, students need to keep careful, detailed, thorough notes about it and why it is important.

We also want students to research themselves as writers and learners so that they can begin to take charge of their own learning before high school. There are many important questions they can consider.

- What conditions do they need in order to write?
- How can they teach themselves to use time efficiently in school and out?
- What types of entries or certain genres do they tend to use for writing?
- What do they do to get "unstuck"?
- How does literature inform their writing?
- Who are their mentors?
- Where are their strengths as writers?
- Where are their weaknesses and how do they plan to remedy them?
- How do they use the rules of language structures to clarify intent?
- How do they use punctuation to manipulate meaning?
- Are they developing a writing style?
- Can they identify characteristics of their writing?

The questions are a few among many that teachers can ask. The goal is simply to have students approach writing in a more conscious, directed manner.

The Notebook for Research across Disciplines

We would like to see the notebooks used throughout the day in middle schools. This requires the support and cooperation of colleagues in other departments. This joint effort would help unite the separate parts of the middle school day. There are topics in social studies or science that would inform a student's writing life. The types of thinking used in math can help students organize and evaluate their writing. We envision students responding to content area material in their writer's notebooks with the idea of developing writing pieces. Thoughtful reflections on science and history have led to many novels, poems, and essays. Why not lead students to the same experience?

Students could use notebook entries to force connections between disciplines. For example, a seventh grader read *The Miracle Worker* by William Gibson. She concluded that Helen's parents were very algebraic because they were bound by laws and could see no answers beyond concrete equations. However, Anne Sullivan was "living in" higher math, because she could see possibilities and creativity and what *could be*, not what was. A group of eighth graders used scientific thinking to investigate literature. They formed a hypothesis about the way two particular authors used tension in their books, and then they tested the hypothesis by searching for and recording evidence from the authors' novels. Finally they drew conclusions after examining their data, which they had recorded in their notebooks.

Using the notebook across disciplines also helps students find a historical context for their writing. How does their thinking fit into the world? How is it different from the ways people thought twenty, forty, ninety years ago? Reflection on content area work within the writer's notebook helps students see learning as a unified whole that is consistent with middle school philosophy.

Keeping writers' notebooks as the foundation for writing in the classroom can lead students to experience the writing life the way many professional writers do. It is certainly not the only way writers work, but it does fit well into the world of school. As teachers, we hope to get the most mileage from everything we do in our classrooms; the time we have with each class is short and there is so much to teach. Elevating the use of the notebook above a mere journal or daily writing practice makes sense as we look for ways to show middle school students that their thinking matters and that school can help them find and take a place in the real world. Ultimately we hope not only to ground middle school students in solid learning habits but also to give them wings to soar to meaningful and creative heights.

Suggested Readings

Bomer, R. (1995). *Time for meaning: Crafting literate lives in middle and high school.* Portsmouth, NH: Heinemann.

Calkins, L. M. (1994). *The art of teaching writing.* Portsmouth, NH: Heinemann.

Fletcher, R. (1996). *A writer's notebook: unlocking the writer within you.* New York: Avon Books.

Fletcher, R. (1996). *Breathing in, breathing out: Keeping a writer's notebook.* Portsmouth, NH: Heinemann.

Janet Angellilo is a literacy staff developer with the Teachers College, Columbia University Reading and Writing Project. She works on implementing literacy reform with elementary and middle school teachers in New York City and other urban areas. A former middle school English teacher, she is currently a doctoral candidate at Teachers College and has been published in *Primary Voices K–6*. Her primary area of interest is helping middle school students become fluent readers and writers.

Anna Danon Reduce is currently a literacy staff developer at Teachers College Reading and Writing Project, where she works with teachers throughout the metropolitan New York area and across the country. As a teacher in Tenafly, New Jersey, she hosted many teachers from the region in her writing/reading workshops. Reduce received her BA from Fordham College and her MTA from Fordham University. She has presented at NCTE and at Teachers College Reading and Writing Project Reunions. She was published in the August 1999 issue of *Primary Voices*.

III The Nature and Needs of Students at the Middle Level

What kind of educational program best helps young adolescents bridge the difficult years between the ages of ten and fourteen?

How can we help these young people become vital contributors to all of the communities of which they are a part?

What is the role of interdisciplinary teaming at the middle level?

How can we guarantee adult mentors for each adolescent?

What does a middle level teacher really need to know before facing a classroom for the first time?

How can middle level educators make certain that their curriculum is a bridge from elementary school to high school?

In this section, five educators, who all have focused on middle level classrooms, answer these questions as they discuss some of the principal components in the education of young adolescents: knowledge about their cognitive and affective needs, the key role of advisory, the function of interdisciplinary teaming, the essential contribution of service learning, the development of sound teacher-preparation programs, and the potential of vertical articulation.

In "The Middle Schooler" Jim Johnston describes the most important element in the classroom, the middle level student. Jim examines both the diversity of young adolescents and the diversity of the programs that will best meet their needs.

Martha Magner discusses two vital programs at the middle level, the advisory and service learning, and explores how each is particularly suited to the needs of the young adolescent. In "A Habit of the Heart: Service Learning," Martha explains how young people can become more connected to their larger community through service to others. Her "Advisory: Building Relationships" defines not only what an advisory program is but also the specific role of the teacher as an advisor.

Lois Stover views middle level education and the middle level student through the lens of interdisciplinary teaming and includes a list of valuable resources. "Interdisciplinary Teaming in the Middle School" offers a fascinating look at what Lois calls "one of the most important distinguishing features of the true middle school" and of the camaraderie present at the first Middle School Mosaic.

Judith A. Hayn shares the early results of an ongoing survey about teacher preparation at the middle undertaken by the CEE Commission on Middle Grades English Language Arts Teacher Education and a bibliography for middle level educators compiled by Lisa A. Spiegel. "Middle Level Teacher Preparation" offers a first look at what educators in the classroom and at the university level expect from our preservice programs in middle level English language arts.

Lanny van Allen concludes the section by reflecting on the potential of coordinating the curriculum, K through 12, which she advocates beginning at the middle level. In "Vertical Connections" Lanny explores how the middle level educators can assume a proactive, linking role in curriculum construction rather than one in which they simply react to the requirements of the elementary and high schools.

Whether you begin reading at the first article or jump into the middle, the essays in this section will introduce you to life at the middle level as visualized by five insightful participants of the first Middle School Mosaic.

11 The Middle Schooler

Jim Johnston
Tolland Middle School, Tolland, Connecticut

Early adolescent, pre-adolescent, young adolescent, transescent, pubescent, and middle schooler are just some of the labels students between the ages of ten and fourteen wear. There are a multitude of additional terms used to describe this group, for example, Hormones Are Us. This group is just as hard to identify and quantify as it is to label. Every audience seeks a simple definition and real parameters for this group. As Linda Robinson states, "Adult in many ways, yet children at heart; independent, yet seeking guidance, support, and love; full of confidence, bravado, and spunk, yet shy and tentative inside, middle school students are a walking set of opposites"(1998, p. 3).

Diverse Students

Physically, this is the time of most change in the human body since birth. Never again will the body change so rapidly. The growth spurt usually occurs at this time, with both height and weight changing fast. Often we teachers are shocked to find that our little sixth graders have become giant seventh graders over the summer vacation. Although these changes continue throughout the year, we teachers see the students on a daily basis and therefore we do not note the changes as clearly as we do upon their return in September. This rapid growth leads to awkwardness, some motor deficiencies, and restlessness that create problems with attention spans. Teachers must be careful to consider this aspect of adolescent development when choosing reading assignments and the activities to accompany them. Full-period discussions are going to cost us some of our students who are too busy growing to pay attention. Research also has shown that this is the time of highest cholesterol levels within the body, which can lead to "brown outs" or lapses in attentiveness lasting between sixty and ninety seconds. Repetition is helpful in these cases. Another of the obvious physical changes is the onset of puberty, which can be an object of concern both for those who have experienced it and those who seem to be waiting endlessly for it to come to them. One outgrowth of this physical change is erratic behavior, which is inconsistent at best. The middle schooler can be adult-like one minute and child-like the next.

Intellectual development also causes great change within each of the children. This is the time of the lowest rate of growth in new brain cells, with the boys' rate three times lower than the girls. This slowed rate means that this age group learns more easily through concrete rather than abstract methods. Listening seems to be the least efficient way of learning at this age. A wide range of approaches is necessary to address the widely varying learning styles. Educators need to address adolescents' short attention span by setting immediate goals, as adolescents often tend to lose sight of long-term goals. Also, heterogeneous grouping favors the use of widespread techniques to address the diverse learning styles of students. As they move to more abstract levels of thought, they are more challenged to use all of their styles of learning to handle these new concepts. Middle schoolers begin working at the concrete level as they enter the middle school; however they leave at a level that uses the higher-order thinking skills as they develop into abstract thinkers.

Socially there are also great changes. The biggest is the increased influence of the peer group. Social acceptance can become the predominate concern for this age group, though it is not necessarily true for all students. Students are particularly sensitive to peer expectations both in the social as well as the academic arenas. The middle school is the social center of these students' lives. Many students come to school for the sole purpose of socializing. For this group any learning is only secondary. Just as the peer group gains much control there are also the beginnings of conflict. Students want to be part of the inside group, but at the same time they want to maintain their own identity. This presents problems that often lead to various conflicts. Students argue with parents about everything, with teachers about anything, and with other peers about social issues. Their desire to be a part of the "in" crowd is fueled by the evil nature of maliciousness directed by the majority at those considered to be on the outside of the group. As these students progress through the middle school years, they begin to move away from the "I" centeredness of their lives to a more global fairness involvement. They form the groups that will become the crusading teens of high school and college. If the right group is involved, they rally around projects to help within the community with a zeal that is beyond belief.

Emotional development is another area of rapid change for this age group. They are beginning to cope more often with a wider variety of emotions. Often they misunderstand their or someone else's emotions, situations that can lead to conflicts. They tend to exaggerate. Some deal from the position of the "crisis of the moment." Life and death are constant concerns as they deal with the world. Behavior is erratic because young adolescents generally lack the confidence necessary to be consistent. A gradual sophistication sets in as they go through eighth grade, which brings a little settling compared to the exaggerated emotions of the seventh grader. However, there continue to be impending disasters that must provoke actions. If you are able to establish a level of trust with these students, you will find out a lot more than you ever wanted to know. Because they seem so insecure, they need someone in whom they can confide, someone who is not going to tell them how they should solve all of their problems. These students seek to be independent, but they also want to be able to seek advice as they try to deal with life.

Diverse Curriculum

These characteristics provide us with ample sources of reading material for our classes. Many books allow students to see that they are not alone by offering insights into how the heroes or heroines solve some of the same issues troubling their own lives. The best thing about this is that these problems can be traced through historical novels as well as into the future with science fiction. The difficulty, however, is that seldom are any two students at the same place in their developmental stages within the classroom. This disparity can present a problem as well as a blessing. It can pose a problem for the child who is a slower developer and may not know anything about the issues being discussed. It can often be a blessing because you can also have someone who is through or nearly through the same stage and can address the issue from the perspective of personal experience. You should also keep your activities brief and active. As they progress through the grades, these learning activities can be extended according to attention span, but they will probably still have to be varied. There will be times when you question their attention span. The same student who can spend little more than a fifteen-minute silent reading time will be entranced with e-mail for an hour or two. Such involvement should be your clue to the types of activity upon which to focus as you share your reading.

If you are searching for the typical middle schooler, so that you can address the needs of this age group, cease your search right now. You will save yourself great amounts of time and frustration. There is no such student. There are the characteristics mentioned above, but all are not overtly experienced by all students in this age range. Nor are these characteristics experienced to the same degree by each student. You do need to become aware of these characteristics so that you can use them in your planning of lessons as well as during your lessons. Being aware of these characteristics and being able to use them to your advantage will make your teaching that much more effective within the classroom.

References

Carnegie Council on Adolescent Development. (1989). *Turning points: Preparing American youth for the 21st century.* Washington, DC: The Council.

Freeman, C. (1996). *Living with a work in progress: A parent's guide to surviving adolescence.* Columbus, OH: National Middle School Association.

National Middle School Association. (1992). *This we believe.* Columbus, OH: National Middle School Association.

Robinson, L. (1998). Understanding middle school students. In K. Beers & B. Samuels (Eds.), *Into focus: Understanding and creating middle school readers.* Norwood, MA: Christopher-Gordon.

Jim Johnston is the language arts specialist in the Tolland Connecticut Middle School and an adjunct faculty member in the reading department of Central Connecticut State University. He has been involved with middle school education and students for his entire thirty-year career. In addition to serving on the executive board for the Connecticut Council of Teachers of English, he is also on the board of the Junior High/Middle School Assembly. He has written many articles and presented numerous papers at various conferences. Johnston is co-editor of the Connecticut Council of Teachers of English newsletter.

12 A Habit of the Heart: Service Learning

Martha M. Magner
MacArthur Barr Middle School, Nanuet, New York

Since 1991, the A. MacArthur Barr Middle School in Nanuet, New York, has offered students in grade eight a service learning program they can take during the quarter in which the student is ordinarily assigned to a Home and Careers class. Service Learning, a program that allows community-based organizations to reach out to young adolescents, creates a positive role at this critical point in the students' lives. The Home and Careers teacher implemented this particular program with the approval of the New York State Department of Education. The stated purposes of this program are

1. to offer service to the student's own community.
2. to provide students the opportunity to apply skills and knowledge learned in the Home and Careers curriculum to real life situations.
3. to create conditions by which students feel known and are a part of something.
4. to allow for greater interaction with people and greater independence among people.
5. to provide leadership opportunities.

How It Works

Students spend the first week of the quarter learning about the program and the skills that will be needed at various sites. These sites include the elementary school, day care centers, nursery school, a school for severely physically and mentally handicapped children, and a nursing home. Before any assignments are made, the students are asked to rank their choices of a placement, and every effort is made to place the student at his first or second choice. No more than two students are placed at one time. As soon as the placements are determined, the students are bused to each site five days a week for about an hour each day for the remainder of the quarter. Scheduled time at the site is achieved by placing the service learning time either before or after a recess or activity time so that the students do not miss any academic time.

Action

At the elementary school, the students assist the teachers with whole-class activities, one-on-one tutoring, art activities, bookmaking, and media productions. At the day care centers, they help the young children with art activities, read to them, and often oversee hygiene care. The nursery school activities are similar, but, in addition, the students help with circle games, singing, and dancing. At the school for physically and mentally handicapped children, the students assist with exercise, eating, puppet shows, academic work, and socialization. Those assigned to the nursing home help transport the patients, serve lunch, play games, draw sketches of seniors, and engage them in conversation. One of the most important elements of the program is that the students are always interacting with people and not just doing isolated tasks that would soon become meaningless for them. Instead, they are performing a needed service for a fellow human being.

Reflection

During their stay at the sites, the students are also scheduled for a reflection period at least twice each week. Reflection is an integral part of the service learning process. Trained teachers work with groups of about ten students to direct and encourage them to think about their experiences during the week and to formulate conclusions in terms of the effects the week's experiences have had on them and the people with whom they interact on a daily basis. They are encouraged to share both their feelings and concerns with the group. In addition, each student is required to keep a daily journal recounting the day's experiences, feelings, and reactions. At the end of the service learning experience, each student is responsible for a major project depicting his or her feelings about the experience at the site. The individual student may choose from various forms of presentation, including essays, videos with written explanation, photographic essays with written explanations, audiotapes with script, a manual for those students who will spend some time at the site in the future, a collage of people and activities at the site with written and oral explanation, case studies of people at a site, and oral histories of seniors at the nursing home. These projects and presentations become a part of the evaluation process by the teacher, the site supervisor, and the other students.

Why Service?

Young adolescents are at an ideal age to experience the satisfaction that providing service to another human being can bring. Receiving recognition for academic achievement and/or athletic accomplishments is commonplace in a society that places competition above cooperation. However, schools can be a microcosm of society and as such can require of the students that which the community will require of them to succeed as adults—compassion, responsiveness to community needs, charity, tolerance, concern for the elderly, responsibility, respect for others, and a willingness to share one's time and talents. If these characteristics are to be an integral part of our future world, then the teachers must send clear messages to students that these are special traits to be valued. We can teach students the relationship among volunteerism, good citizenship, and the continuing maintenance of society. The development of the healthy element of service learning in a school will help open doors to change and communication among students, teachers, and the real world in which they live. It is a way to develop habits of the heart that cannot be measured by standardized tests but that start each student on his or her journey to a rewarding future.

Listen to these students' comments about service learning:

> I loved service learning at the nursery school and I wish I could take service learning all year.

> My service learning experience at the preschool has really been a fun experience. It has taught me that all people are different.

> By working with children at the elementary school, it gave me a little feeling of what it is like to be a teacher.

> Serving at the preschool has been a great learning experience. Because of my interaction with the kids, my patience and my leadership abilities have grown a great deal.

> Whenever I'm at the school for the handicapped children, I get a real good feeling inside of me. It seems I'm making a real difference in the kids' lives and that I am really appreciated there. The great thing about this experience is that not only did I have a great time with my class, but that I also learned life skills.

From the students' statements, you can see that service learning is an excellent opportunity for students to learn and develop as they make steps toward mature, adult life.

References

Carnegie Corporation. (1992). *A Matter of Time*. New York: Carnegie Corporation.

Fertman, C. I., White, G. P., & White, L. J. (1996). *Service learning in the middle school: Building a culture of service*. Columbus, OH: National Middle School Association.

George, P. S., & Alexander, W. M. (1993). *The exemplary middle school*. (2nd ed.). New York: Harcourt, Brace, Jovanovich College Division.

National Helpers Network. (1998). *Reflection: The Key to Service Learning*. (2nd ed.). New York: National Helpers Network, INC.

*　　*　　*　　*　　*

Don't overlook the entire November 1996 edition of the *Middle School Journal* (vol. 28 [2]), which is completely devoted to service learning.

Martha M. Magner is the District Testing Coordinator for the Nanuet School District in Rockland County, New York, and an adjunct professor for the College of Mount St. Vincent. She has taught in this district for the past twenty-eight years, twenty of which were at the A. MacArthur Barr Middle School, a New York School of Excellence. She was one of the original founders of the advisory program in this school and later helped implement a service learning program as an integral part of the curriculum for eighth graders. Magner is active in NCTE and in the International Reading Association as a member of the Adolescent Literacy Commission. She is also a member of the National Middle School Association and has made many presentations for the three organizations.

13 Interdisciplinary Teaming in the Middle School

Lois T. Stover
St. Mary's College, St. Mary's City, Maryland

As a teacher educator and former teacher of English and drama at the middle level, I am interested in the concept of the interdisciplinary team as it functions in the middle school. The interdisciplinary team organization is one of the most important distinguishing features of the true middle school and serves as a keystone for its structure, helping all of the other elements that create a middle school environment to work together and function smoothly.

Key Components of Teaming in the Middle

To begin discussion of this concept at the Middle School Mosaic we created a structured web on the concept of "team," brainstorming synonyms, positive associations, negative associations, and kinds of teams we have experienced in our lives outside schools. Our list of responses included items such as collaboration, shared experience, common goals/vision, individual strengths, the idea that "the whole is larger than the sum of the parts." We also commented that one weak link can disable a team, noting that egos, conflicting personalities, lack of time to share and create vision together, impositions from outside the team such as assessment mandates and requirements contrary to the team's own goals can all adversely affect the effectiveness of any team, whether a sports team, team of workers in a factory or restaurant, collaborative group in a graduate class, a family, or a group working on a dramatic and musical production.

Next, we identified the following key features of the knowledge and skills required of middle school teachers. Teachers at the middle level need

- to know the students
- to plan accordingly for interdisciplinary instruction

- to recognize the importance of making gradual transitions for students between elementary and high school
- to reduce unnecessary stress on students
- to recognize the importance of more guidance in the affective domain for younger adolescents than is typically provided for them in the junior high school model

Given the demands placed on teachers of middle school students, as well as the ways in which teaming of any sort allows for shared responsibility and for the use of the individual's strengths in service to the group's goals, teaming seems a logical strategy for organizing instruction at the middle level. As Wiles and Bondi (1993) state in *The Essential Middle School,* "Team teaching (or teaming) is a type of instructional organization in which two or more teachers pool their resources, interests, expertise, and knowledge of students and take joint responsibility for meeting a significant part of the instructional needs of the same group of students" (p. 103). Therefore, teaming for instruction within the middle school often means that

- a sense of belonging for both teachers and students is created
- maximum use is made of teacher strengths
- teachers and students are clustered in the same physical area of the building
- teachers are able to work with small groups, individuals, and large groups
- teachers can share their insights, pool their resources, develop ideas collaboratively, and make life easier and more meaningful for students. (Homework/testing; relevance through interdisciplinary connections)

It is important to note that—as is true for any team seeking to accomplish a shared goal—team teaching *demands* common instructional time and shared planning time. Without attention to the need to collaborate in the planning and delivery of instruction, as well as in conferencing about students and their individual needs, team teaching will not work.

Individuals interested in what teaming looks like in use might read an excellent description of "best practices" in the area of team organization options (George & Alexander, 1993, pp. 257–65). Based on our own experiences, participants of this round-table discussion noted that members of middle level teams engage in the following activities as they seek to share their resources, energy, and vision to create positive learning environments and experiences for their students:

- scheduling classes

- developing patterns of grouping for student instruction within the team
- selecting and developing curricular plans and resources for implementation
- correlating curriculum and instruction from different subject areas to ensure maximum effectiveness
- allocating space
- dispersing budget
- using blocks of time
- selecting new staff (new teachers must be compatible with team members)
- making contacts with parents as a team
- placing students in programs to address individual needs
- orienting new students/generating collaborative and shared expectations
- cooperating with teachers of "specials"
- generating "exploratories" in response to both student need and faculty expertise

Thematically Based Interdisciplinary Instruction

Next, we also explored more particularly the concept of thematically based interdisciplinary instruction. The key point that emerged from this part of the discussion was that such instruction should be thematically based around *concepts* broad enough to promote exploration of that theme from multiple dimensions, thus allowing students to be engaged in creating patterns and thereby increasing their depth of understanding. We generated a list of activities and issues of importance to middle school students and from these generalized larger "themes" around which interdisciplinary instruction can be based. For example, middle school students spend a good deal of time either on the phone or passing notes. We can tap this interest by creating an interdisciplinary unit on "communication." Our students are concerned about how to adjust as they make the transition from childhood to adulthood, making "change" a rich possible interdisciplinary topic for exploration. For anyone who has ever taught or parented a middle level student, the fact that tempers are short, that tension is often high between student and adult is self-evident. Allowing students to explore their feelings from multiple perspectives through a unit on "conflict" would be useful.

We identified the key to interdisciplinary planning as asking questions at the unit level that students can then attempt to answer by bringing to bear all the resources and strategies of various content areas. Thus, the unit level questions for a unit on "patterns" might be something like "Why do patterns exist? Why do individuals seek to create and then follow patterns?" Each content area has something to offer as students explore these questions. In English/language arts, students can explore patterns of narrative vs. other kinds of writing, language usage patterns, or patterns inherent in different forms of poetry reflective of various cultures. Social studies teachers can help students see the way the pendulum swings on issues of public policy over time, the patterns inherent in a country's march toward revolution or civil war, economic trends, or voting patterns. In math, students can be exposed to patterns in geometry, patterns involved in solving certain kinds of problems, or concepts like Fibonacci numbers, while in science, the patterns of change as the earth's tectonic plates move and shift, as rock of various kinds forms, as crystals grow, as carbon dioxide changes to oxygen and then back again can be investigated, or students can study various cycles of life. Discussion of the ways in which visual artists and musicians use patterns, the patterns involved in playing well offensively or defensively in various team sports, and patterns of disease can take place in the various "specials" such as art, physical education, and health, thus making students see connections across disciplinary boundaries and allowing them to view the topic in a multifaceted way. If such instruction is coupled with attention during advisory or guidance/homeroom sessions to self-analysis of patterns of behavior and goal setting, then the middle school student's entire school day becomes interconnected and thus more meaningful.

As we discussed our own favorite interdisciplinary topics, ranging from survival to war to environments, we once again agreed that such instructional programming mandates shared planning time and a commitment at the school level to the teaming concept. We noted that conflicting personalities, the demands of state tests that do not honor interdisciplinary exploration, and lack of parental/student understanding of the overall vision can interfere with effective use of teams. But, we also agreed that it is possible to work within the confines of whatever situation exists in a particular school, that it is possible to "start small," and to self–educate. What follows is a list of some of the resources that individuals have found particularly useful in trying to move into interdisciplinary team teaching at the middle level.

References

Beane, J. (1990). *A middle school curriculum: From rhetoric to reality*. Columbus, OH: National Middle School Association.

Beane, J. (1993). Problems and possibilities for an integrative curriculum. *Middle School Journal, 25* (1), 18–23.

George, P., & Alexander, W. M. (1993). *The exemplary middle school*. (2nd ed.). New York: Harcourt, Brace, Jovanovich College Division.

Jacobs, H. H. (Ed.). (1989). *Interdisciplinary curriculum: Design and implementation*. Alexandria, VA: Association for Supervision and Curriculum Development.

Lounsbury, J. H. (Ed). (1992). *Connecting the curriculum through interdisciplinary instruction*. Columbus, OH: National Middle School Association.

Pate, P. E., Homestead, E. R., & McGinnis, K. (1997). *Making integrated curriculum work: Teachers, students, and the quest for coherent curriculum*. New York: Columbia Teachers College Press.

Stover, L. T. (1996). *Young adult literature: The heart of the middle school curriculum*. Portsmouth, NH: Boynton/Cook.

Wiles, J., & Bondi, J. (1993). *The essential middle school*. (2nd ed). New York: Macmillan.

Lois T. Stover is professor and Chair of Educational Studies at St. Mary's College of Maryland. She teaches courses in children's and adolescent literature, teaching methodology at the secondary level, and educational psychology. As an active member of NCTE, Stover has served as the chair of both the CEE Commission on Middle Grades English Language Arts Teacher Education and of ALAN. A former teacher of English at the high school level, Stover "saw the light" and taught English and drama to middle school students for three years, delighting in her students' enthusiasm and eagerness to learn.

14 Advisory: Building Relationships

Martha M. Magner
MacArthur Barr Middle School, Nanuet, New York

Elliot Eisner has said, "It is not the job of the schools to prepare kids for school. It is the job of the schools to prepare kids for life." How our middle schools respond to the developmental needs of young adolescents will affect just what kind of adults they become and provide them with basic ingredients for living. Among these are how to deal with anxiety, how to make friends, how to resolve conflicts and make decisions, and how to love and be loved. It can easily be seen then that a central feature of any middle school is the fourth "R"—relationships.

Defining the Advisory

The quality of relationships between students and teachers should be based on caring, respect, responsibility, and mutual understanding. For the ten- to fifteen-year-old, it is most important that there be a positive social interaction between a student and at least one adult in the school. Their changing relationships with other adults, especially their parents, along with the increasing importance of their peers makes it imperative for middle schools to encourage positive adult interaction and also positive peer interaction. These positive interactions can be facilitated by an advisor-advisee program as an integral part of the students' day.

Advisory is not a form of therapy, nor even of counseling; rather, it is simply an opportunity for students to touch base with a concerned adult for a short time each day and have the opportunity to request help on any matters of any concern. Help might be offered on the best way to approach a long-term assignment, an upcoming test, or a problem the student has with a particular teacher. Students may seek advice on how best to organize their school day, their out-of-school day, or their school materials. Problems with peers may also be discussed. Much of the time spent in Advisory will involve group discussions relating to the topics above or other topics of concern to the students. However, when confronted with problems of a serious nature, advisors must refer the students to the school guidance counselor, the school psychologist, or the school administration.

Advisory is a statement to the student that there is an adult who cares, someone who will listen, who is not a judge, and who will be there for the student when the need arises. The advisor is by no means a substitute for the trained guidance counselor. Instead, he or she is there to assist the young adolescents in their relationships and daily decision making. First and foremost, the advisor must be an effective teacher who possesses a knowledge of the needs and characteristics of the young adolescent and who has a genuine liking for these students.

Although literature on middle level education emphasizing the need for a strong advisory program has been available for about forty years, it has only been in the past ten to fifteen years that this program has become nationally known. Both the National Middle School Association and the National Association of Secondary School Principals have asserted the need for this program. The Carnegie Council on Adolescent Development states in its report that all middle level schools need to have "small group advisories that ensure that every student is well known by at least one adult" (1989, p. 40). The report also points out that the middle school may well be the student's last best chance to avoid a diminished future. It is at this time that the students must learn the strategies to deal with problems in a productive way. This report also recognizes the challenge to convince the American public and school boards and administrators to transform middle schools from places that fail to prepare our youth for their future to places that strive for success for all students.

Structuring a Successful Advisory Program

Since the growth of this type of program has been slow to take hold even after being adjudged critical, one wonders why the implementation has not been more successful nationwide. What does it take to make an advisory program work? Primarily, the program must be based on true student needs and/or concerns, not on the way an adult perceives the needs. The successful program exists in the school in which the administration provides ongoing support. The counselor serves as the key resource person, materials are readily available, and the mechanism exists to support the continued evolution of the program. Most middle school teachers already possess a genuine concern for the students they teach, the most necessary quality for the good advisor. If administrators mandate the advisory program without the support of the teachers, research has shown that the program will probably fail.

In addition, a very important ingredient to the success of a program is continuous caring about students as a core value of the school. Advisors become advocates for their students across the entire day, take special care of their students, and relate to these students in a very personal way. The advisor treats each student in a special manner, establishes rapport, and shares feelings.

A successful advisory program has a clear focus, wherein an advisor develops a special relationship with each advisee and works with the group to help them understand themselves and others and to cope with and be happy in their world. All the activities must implement the affective goal established. The good advisor observes his or her students each day, noting who participates in discussions, whether someone monopolizes discussions, who is sad, who is moping, who is scared, and who just needs to know that someone cares. These observations are often the content for the day's meeting, whether it be with the whole group or a single student.

Advisory requires a specific block of time that cannot be used for other activities, announcements, or classes. At the beginning of each school year, advisory is a time in which school adjustment and group identity should be attended to first in order to cultivate a sense of cohesiveness and readiness for all that is to follow. It is accomplished by eliminating the students' concerns about new programs, new teachers, a new building, new schedules, new subjects, and even new lockers. Then, too, cohesiveness and trust that lead to a sense of identity with an advisor and the group must be established from the start. If the foundation is strong, then the themes and activities can be developed. As the students mature, there must be new themes and activities directed to the new and often diverse levels of maturity. Advisors should be encouraged to infuse unique experiences into the program and be aware that each Advisory takes on a unique personality.

In addition to group support, there must be staff development. Just giving advisors binders full of materials will not do the job. The best staff development emphasizes student concerns, provides demonstrations of various methods, includes discussions of the activities and methods used by advisors, and shows how to assess success. Advisors need to learn how to deal with the everyday concerns of the students in a positive way, ensuring each student that all discussions remain a part of that advisory. The advisor must be aware that no matter how trivial a problem seems, it is often monumental to the young adolescent. Although middle school students are in the throes of developing a sense of identity, they are nevertheless at a stage in which they are cognitively unable to intellectualize emotional situations. Only then will advisees feel free to discuss needs and concerns, seek help, and often help each other. In addition, there must be a process in place for handling serious problems a student brings to his/her advisor. When the advisor must seek additional help from the guidance counselor, the psychologist, or the administrator, it will only be successful if the student trusts the advisor and is part of the solution. Finally, administrators should establish a back-up support system of a schoolwide advisory coordinating committee in which the advisors can meet to discuss and brainstorm the best methods of achieving success with an advisory.

Advisory is the best part of the day for those who are truly involved with their advisees. Addressing the students' affective needs will help these students throughout their lifetimes and enable them to deal effectively with whatever life holds for them.

References

Carnegie Council on Adolescent Development. (1989). *Turning points: Preparing American youth for the 21st century: Recommendations for transforming middle grade schools*. Washington, D.C.: Carnegie Corporation.

Cole, C. G. (1992). *Nurturing a teacher advisory program*. Columbus, OH: National Middle School Association.

Doda, N., Hoversten, C., & Lounsbury, J. H. (1991). *Treasure chest: A teacher advisory source*. Columbus, OH: National Middle School Association.

Galassi, J. P., Gulledge, S. A., & Cox, N. D. (1998). *Advisory: Definitions, description, decisions, and directions*. Columbus, OH: National Middle School Association.

James, M. (1986). *Advisor-advisee programs: Why, what, and how?* Columbus, OH: National Middle School Association.

Wiles, J., & Bondi, J. (1993). *The essential middle school*. (2nd ed.). New York: Macmillan.

Martha M. Magner is the District Testing Coordinator for the Nanuet School District in Rockland County, New York, and an adjunct professor for the College of Mount St. Vincent. She has taught in this district for the past twenty-eight years, twenty of which were at the A. MacArthur Barr Middle School, a New York School of Excellence. She was one of the original founders of the advisory program in this school and later helped implement a service learning program as an integral part of the curriculum for eighth graders. Magner is active in NCTE and in the International Reading Association as a member of the Adolescent Literacy Commission. She is also a member of the National Middle School Association and has made many presentations for the three organizations.

15 Middle Level Teacher Preparation

Judith A. Hayn
Loyola University, Chicago, Illinois

The Conference on English Education Commission on Middle Grades English Language Arts Teacher Education has an ongoing collaboration with the Junior High/Middle School Assembly. By uniting our efforts to improve teacher preparation programs in the middle grades, classroom teachers and university/college educators stand firm in this commitment to support the best teaching practices by both groups. This results in quality English language arts teaching no matter what the level.

The commission takes its charge very seriously. While those of us who teach middle school courses at colleges and universities may be restricted by individual state certification or endorsement procedures, the needs of the early adolescent remain at the forefront of what we do to prepare teachers in our discipline to deal with this important age group. As Jeff Wilhelm reminds us in *Standards in Practice: Grades 6–8* (1996), the junior high is "where we keep them or lose them."

Background

In Detroit at the annual NCTE Fall Convention as part of the first Middle School Mosaic, the commission began the dissemination of a survey for middle level classroom teachers. The survey asked for input about the necessity for separate middle school (grades 5–8) certification where possible. The survey contained questions about the importance of specific preparation backgrounds where separate certification is not an option.

Data was collected at various sessions of the Middle School Mosaic, at a morning social for middle level teachers and teacher educators, and at the Junior High/Middle School's information table in the exhibit hall. Subsequent surveys were conducted in Albuquerque at the Spring Conference and in Nashville at the Fall Convention in 1998.

CEE Commission on Middle School English Language Arts Teacher Preparation: Survey

Please complete this brief survey and return to any middle school program presenter.

1. Should teachers from the middle level receive a certificate specifically for middle school (grades 5–8) teaching?   Yes____ No____

2. If a state does not have a separate middle level certificate, are middle level teachers better served by certifying at the elementary level or secondary (high) school?

   Either

   Elementary ____   Secondary ____   Elementary or Secondary ____

3. Which of the following courses are essential in a quality middle school certification program?

Not Essential		Essential		Very Essential
1	2	3	4	5

   Introduction to Psychology _____
   Educational Psychology _____
   Exceptionality/Special Education _____
   Multicultural Education _____
   Foundations of Education _____
   Adolescent Development _____
   Instructional Design _____
   Methods of Teaching (in the Middle School) _____
   Discipline and Management _____
   Children's/Adolescent Literature _____
   Middle School Organization/Program _____

4. What experiences are absolutely essential in a quality middle level certification program?

Not Essential		Essential		Very Essential
1	2	3	4	5

   Field experiences in middle school _____
   Tutoring in middle school _____
   Team teaching _____
   Interdisciplinary planning of units _____
   Visits to true middle schools and comparison with junior high organizations _____

5. What knowledge base is essential to the quality middle level certification program that differentiates it from the elementary and high school programs?

Results

The following results reveal opinions fascinating in their diversity—not wholly unexpected considering the variety of students and teachers in various parts of the country. It is important to note that not all of the questions were answered by all of the respondents. Those who favor secondary preparation make up not quite half the almost 90 respondents while another 40 percent think it does not matter, with a small number preferring elementary backgrounds for middle level educators.

CEE Commission on Middle School English Language Arts Teacher Preparation: 1999 Survey Results

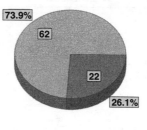

1. Should teachers from the middle level receive a certificate specifically for middle school (grades 5–8) teacher? Yes _____ No _____

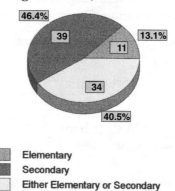

2. If a state does not have a separate middle level certificate, are middle level teachers better served by certifying at the elementary level or secondary (high) school?

The essential coursework current middle school language arts practitioners selected reveals an interesting pattern. Ranking each course on a scale of 1–5, with 5 representing "Very Essential" and 1 as "Not Essential," those college courses stressing Adolescent Development drew the strongest support. Other classes deemed vital included Methods of Teaching (in the Middle School), Children's/Adolescent Literature, and Discipline and Management, with support for Middle School Organization/Program coursework. Teachers saw Introduction to Psychology, Educational Psychology, Exceptionality/Special Education, Multicultural Education, and Foundations of Education as "Essential," but not crucial. Both the Introduction and Foundation's courses were seen as less than "Essential" by more than twenty teachers. Instructional Design supporters were split between those who valued it and those who valued it somewhat.

3. Which of the following courses are essential in a quality middle school certification program?

COURSE	1	2	3	4	5
Introduction to Psychology	7	24	24	11	10
Educational Psychology	2	12	25	18	22
Exceptionality/Special Education		8	25	22	24
Multicultural Education	1	11	23	24	19
Foundations of Education	9	22	21	17	8
Adolescent Development		1	3	7	73
Instructional Design	1	5	14	24	32
Methods of Teaching (in the Middle School)			5	11	67
Discipline and Management			7	16	57
Children's/Adolescent Literature		1	5	16	59
Middle School Organization/Program		4	14	22	40

Column headers: Not Essential = 1; Essential = 3; Very Essential = 5

In dealing with experiences that are absolutely essential for a quality middle level certification program, practitioners indicated that those involving the realities of the classroom were most valued: Field courses in the college curriculum, including Introduction to Psychology, Multicultural Education, Methods of Teaching (for the middle school), and Children's/Adolescent Literature. Teachers were asked what was essential for a future middle school teacher concerning field experiences, tutoring, team teaching, interdisciplinary planning of units, and visitations to compare middle with junior high schools.

4. What experiences are absolutely essential in a quality middle level certification program?

	Not Essential		Essential		Very Essential
	1	2	3	4	5
COURSE	**1**	**2**	**3**	**4**	**5**
Field experiences in middle school	1	1	3	5	73
Tutoring in middle school	3	16	24	12	22
Team teaching	2	4	17	24	35
Interdisciplinary planning of units	1	1	20	24	38
Visits to true middle schools and comparison with junior high organizations	1	6	7	19	47

The last, open-ended question asked teachers to explain the knowledge base they deem crucial to a quality middle level certification program, one that differentiates it from elementary and secondary teacher preparation. The following answers are representative of the varied responses.

5. What knowledge base is essential to the quality middle level certificate program that differentiates it from elementary and high school programs?

> A true middle school engages in the practices of team teaching and flexible scheduling. A certification program should address these practices.

> Programs should be supervised by people who themselves have been mid-level educators and *love* the middle school environment and students.

> Adolescent development, management-style training, willingness to release [authority] and co-create curriculum with students, and team teaching are the key differences in training/preparation.

> Understanding of the middle school student and learning how to teach across disciplines while still having excellent knowledge of the content area.

> Reading instruction and strategies and the psychology of the adolescent learner.

Conclusions

Of the nearly 90 teachers responding, a clear majority favor separate certification for middle level practitioners. A division occurs, however, when the question asked concerns middle level teachers' need of field experiences. Those in middle schools (which did not specify the internship as a component) received the most support, with visits to true middle schools and comparison with junior high organizations acquiring the next. Teachers were divided in the emphasis placed on tutoring, team teaching, and interdisciplinary planning of units from "Essential" to "Very Essential."

The response to the open-ended question "What knowledge base is essential to the quality middle level certification program that differentiates it from the elementary and high school programs?" provided opportunities for varied responses. A perusal of teacher concerns does continue the emphasis revealed above; that is, an understanding of and experiences with adolescent development are vital. Understanding the early adolescent learner is apparently more valuable than content-area knowledge, although a number of teachers mentioned the importance of coursework in reading, reading and writing workshops, young adult literature, and the humanities.

In Nashville, the results of this data collection served as a basis for a working session where university and college instructors were paired with classroom teachers at roundtable discussions. Participants in this session sought to continue solidifying the accuracy of the database and seeking sources for publication of the findings—aiming the conclusions at those involved in educational leadership. The commission stresses a joining of all those interested in middle school teacher education as the preferred route to finding "best practices," no matter the affiliation.

The Commission on Middle Grades English Language Arts Teacher Education also continues to compile a bibliography of resources for teachers, teacher educators, and administrators with a focus on teacher preparation, staff development, and in-service. An abbreviated list of current recommendations appears at the conclusion of this article with a listing of recent books, journals, sources, and websites designed for both the practitioner and the preservice teacher.

Selected Middle Level Resources

Compiled by Lisa A. Spiegel
University of South Dakota, Vermillion, SD

Allen, H. A., Splittgerber, F. L., & Manning, M. L. (1993). *Teaching and learning in the middle level school.* New York: Maxwell Macmillan.

Arnold, J., & Stevenson, C. (1998). *Teachers' teaming handbook: A middle level planning guide.* Fort Worth, TX: Harcourt, Brace.

Atwell, N. (1998). *In the middle: New understandings about writing, reading, and learning*. Portsmouth, NH: Boynton/Cook.

Beane, J. A. (1997). *Curriculum integration: Designing the core of democratic education*. New York: Teachers College Press.

Carnegie Council on Adolescent Development of the Carnegie Corporation of New York. (1989). *Turning points: Preparing American youth for the 21st century: Recommendations for transforming middle grade schools.* Washington, DC: The Council.

Clark, S. N., & Clark, D. C. (1994). *Restructuring the middle level school: Implications for school leaders*. Albany, NY: State University of New York Press.

Clark, S. N., & Clark, D. C. (1995). *The middle level principal's role in implementing interdisciplinary curriculum*. Reston, VA: National Association of Secondary School Principals.

David, R. (Ed.). (1998). *Moving forward from the past: Early writings and current reflections of middle school founders*. Columbus, OH: NMSA and Pennsylvania Middle School Association.

Forte, I., & Schurr, S. (1996). *Integrating instruction in language arts: Strategies, activities, projects, tools & techniques*. Nashville, TN: Incentive Publications.

George, P. S., & Alexander, W. M. (1993). *The exemplary middle school*. New York: Harcourt Brace.

George, P., Renzulli, J., Reis, S., & Erb, T. (1998). *Dilemmas in talent development in the middle grades: Two views*. Columbus, OH: NMSA.

Hatch, H., & Hytten, K. (1997). *Mobilizing resources for district-wide middle grades reform*. Columbus, OH: NMSA.

Holland, H. (1998). *Making change: Three educators join the battle for better schools*. Portsmouth, NH: Heinemann.

Irvin, J. L. (Ed.). (1997). *What current research says to the middle level practitioner*. Columbus, OH: NMSA.

Irvin, J. L. (1990). *Reading and the middle school student: Strategies to enhance literacy*. Boston: Allyn and Bacon.

Kain, D. (1998). *Camel-makers: Building effective teacher teams together: A modern fable for educators*. Columbus, OH: NMSA.

Lipka, R., Lounsbury, J. H., Toepfer, C., Vars, G., Allessi, S., & Kridel, C. (1998). *The eight-year study revisited: Lessons from the past for the present*. Columbus, OH: NMSA.

McEwin, C. K., & Dickinson, T. S. (1995). *The professional preparation of middle level teachers: Profiles of successful programs*. Columbus, OH: NMSA.

McEwin, C. K., Dickinson, T. S., Erb, T. O., & Scales, P. (1995). *A vision of excellence: Organizing for middle grades teacher preparation*. Columbus, OH: NMSA and Search Institute.

McEwin, C. K., Dickinson, T. S., & Jenkins, D. M. (1996). *America's middle schools: Practices and programs—A 25-year perspective.* Columbus, OH: NMSA.

Moore, K. D. (1999). *Middle and secondary instructional methods.* Boston: McGraw-Hill.

NMSA. (1995). *This we believe: Developmentally responsive middle level schools.* Columbus, OH: NMSA.

NMSA. (1997). *National middle school association/NCATE-approved curriculum guidelines handbook.* Columbus, OH: NMSA.

NMSA. (1997). *Directory of middle level teacher preparation programs.* Columbus, OH: NMSA.

Wheelock, A. (1999). *Safe to be smart: Building a culture for standards-based reform in the middle grades.* Columbus, OH: NMSA.

Wilhelm, J. (1996). *Standards in Practice, Grades 6–8.* Urbana, IL: National Council of Teachers of English.

Journals/Periodicals

Classroom Connections—NMSA
The Family Connection—NMSA
Middle School Journal—NMSA
Middle Ground: The Magazine of Middle Level Education—NMSA
Midpoints—NMSA
Research in Middle Level Education Quarterly—NMSA
Target—NMSA
Voices from the Middle—NCTE

Addresses

National Middle School Association (NMSA)
2600 Corporate Exchange Drive, Suite 370
Columbus, OH 43231
1-800-528-6672
1-614-895-4750 (FAX)

Internet/Websites

NMSA: **www.nmsa.org**

NCTE: **www.ncte.org**

http://www.wnet.org/wnetschool

WNET's practical service for K-12 educators. Designed by teachers, for teachers. Web-based lesson plans, etc.

NMSA's research report #14— "What is the impact of inclusion on students and staff in the middle school setting?"

http://education.indiana.edu/cas

Center for Adolescent Studies

http://ericeece.org
ERIC Clearinghouse on Elementary & Early Childhood Education
http://www.coedu.usf.edu/middlegrades
National Resource Center for Middle Grades Education
http://aj.com
Search Engine
http://www.hoxie.org

Judith A. Hayn is assistant professor in the Department of Curriculum, Instruction, and Educational Psychology at Loyola University, Chicago. She is director of the Sun Belt Writing Project. Hayn has also taught at Auburn University and the University of North Carolina at Wilmington. While pursuing her doctorate at the University of Kansas, she taught English composition at the college level. Hayn has taught in Nebraska and Kansas in both junior and senior high schools. From 1995 to 1998, she served as chair of the CEE Commission on Middle Grades English Language Arts Teacher Education.

16 Vertical Connections

Lanny van Allen
University of Texas, Austin, Texas

E ven though most educators favor a coordinated curriculum in English language arts from grades K through 12, quite honestly, putting up a sign or making an announcement of a session about vertical connectedness or vertical articulation does not draw a large, excited crowd of teachers at conventions and conferences. Such a session, however, does bring some interested and thoughtful teachers. Some of them have envisioned the ideal situation in their districts if the pre-K through 12 (maybe 16) students and parents and community acted together as one to give students the skills and concepts not just for the next grade but for life. They have imagined their districts achieving quality and excellence in education through purposeful and sequential efforts across the grades. Vertical connectedness starts with vertical conversations.

Importance of Vertical Connections

The teachers who come to the sessions tell us everyone knows that vertical connectedness, or curricular coordination, would improve our schools, help our students achieve a quality education, and make teaching a more satisfying profession. If we as teachers know all of those things, then why do we not act on them immediately?

In the sessions, teachers discuss barriers to bringing about vertical connectedness. They always agree that this is one situation for which money, or the lack of it, is *not* a barrier. Even though money is always welcomed, we can actually achieve vertical cooperation without budget increases. That is good news! Some other teachers say their biggest need in achieving vertical cooperation is time—time to talk and share and plan—and that the extra time does mean money, so we list time and money as possible barriers.

One big stumbling block teachers talk about is blame. At a recent meeting of local educators, Dr. Melody Johnson, a former director of the Middle School Division at the Texas Education Agency, shared this silly poem that names everybody who's to blame.

Whose Fault Is It? Certainly Not Mine

The college professor who said, "Such wrong in the student is a
    shame,
Lack of preparation in the high school is to blame

Said the high school teacher, "Good heavens that boy is a fool
The fault, of course, is with the middle school."

The middle school teacher said, "From such stupidity may I be
    spared,
They send him to me so unprepared."

The elementary teacher said, "The kindergartners are blockheads
    all,
They call it preparation, why, it's worse than none at all."

The kindergarten teacher said, "Such a lack of training never
    did I see,
What kind of mother must that woman be!"

The mother said, "That helpless child, he's not to blame
For you see, his father's folks are all the same."

Said the father at the end of the line,
"I doubt the rascal's even mine."

—Anonymous

Teachers in the sessions say that many times they feel defensive when remarks such as these are made: "If students had learned the grammar skills when they were supposed to they wouldn't be doing so badly on the senior test." The press exacerbates the defensive feelings with headlines such as "College Teachers Find Freshmen Lacking in Basic Skills."

Among the list servers on my electronic mail is George Melon, a thirty-year middle school teacher and principal who writes from the University of Nebraska a series called "Up the Middle and up the Middle—Quickly." He is writing not about the university high school disconnection but about the eighth-/ninth-grade grade disconnection. Around the United States, it seems to be a frequent topic: the problem of failing ninth graders.

Whether the ninth grade is in a 7–9 position or a 9–12 position, the problem remains one of transition. Many people have to connect, collaborate, work closely together, plan carefully, and monitor consistently this transition. John Lounsbury and Howard Johnston wrote *How Fares the Ninth Grade?* (1985); however, adequate attention has not been paid, so the challenge continues. M. Cyrene Wells's *Literacies Lost* (1995) sheds significant light on the subject of disconnectedness. Wells "hangs around" with a group of students, and, after they accept her, she writes a story of their last year of middle school and first year of high school. We hear about the transition from the students' point of view. We hope that Wells's ethnographic study is the first of many that will help with the vertical connecting process.

A group of teachers in a vertical articulation session agree that if we are all collaborating and envisioning an almost seamless developmental program for students pre-K through 12 (or 16), that if we are working as a team, helping and supporting and building scaffolds along the way, we could make defensive attitudes go away. They all agree, yes, it is hard work but certainly possible and certainly an uplifting thought!

Some teachers in our group agree that a few teachers may be caught up in the massive work of planning and grading and their own little corner of the world, so caught up that they have difficulty in believing that working with those in the preceding and succeeding grades would bring less stress, more harmony, more success, and more satisfaction.

Visualizing Vertical Connections

Because the challenges/conditions seem to be the major barriers to accomplishing vertical connectedness, where do we begin if we want our co-workers to "visualize vertical connectedness?" One way to begin is for a few teachers (a little time, a little money) to visit a school district in which progress is being made. Or if you go to a session at the next conference, talk to teachers involved in vertical articulation, then communicate with them after you go home. Ask them to tell about what worked—what did not work—for them as they addressed vertical connectedness.

Is there one particular model of vertical cooperation, a plan we can all take home to our campus and talk about? No. (And could this perhaps be interpreted as a barrier? It can certainly be interpreted as a challenge.) In one session at a convention, there are ten teachers in a circle: there are nearly ten "takes"/approaches to vertical cooperation from a local point of view, all of them important! They see them not as barriers but rather as endless possibilities. Begin by inviting a few eighth- and ninth-grade teachers to meet and ask them to decide on just one goal to work on at this time. Later, perhaps invite more people. Or, have one teacher from each grade level from pre-K through 12 (and up) in a feeder-pattern of the district meet together and work on aligning the curriculum.

A poll of freshmen at New York City's Columbia University revealed that the freshmen had said that it should take only about a year and a half to learn all of the "stuff" they had taken twelve years to learn. (Think of all the years we reviewed and revisited the parts of speech and elements of a short story and steps for doing a research paper! Uh, oh, I'm starting to get defensive!) Someone suggests that we would not waste all of that time if we built the curriculum from the ninth grade down; we could then get rid of those gaps and redundancies. Think about it.

I heard it said another way at a different conference: "The most effective staff development is that in which education, K through12, is aligned, and twelfth-grade teachers are communicating with kindergarten teachers about what results would produce a quality graduate ready for the challenges of the twenty-first century."

So perhaps staff development by the "outside expert" or by an insider is an appropriate way to begin in your district. Another way to start is to get a few people from each feeder campus together with a teacher leader or with principals introducing and establishing one goal at a time. Afterward, these teachers could go back and talk it up on their campuses. Or, a few teachers could get together to read *Literacies Lost*, discuss the challenges of transition, and invite a few more teachers to join them.

Another way to begin is to have one or two teachers from each feeder school meet and use, as a guide, a working paper developed by NCTE Elementary, Secondary, and College Sections, 1988–89, for Planning and Articulation by Council Constituencies called "NCTE's Position on the Teaching of English: Assumptions and Practices." For a copy of this paper, visit our Web site at www.ncte.org/positions/assumptions.html. Not only is this paper a significant piece in itself but it also serves as a model for a district that is attempting to achieve connectedness. It is about starting conversations where we are, about eliminating or finding ways to go around the barriers.

Call them whatever you want—pods, vertical teams, pyramids, or feeder-pattern teams. Members of one successful vertical team here in Austin say that they began by imagining the graduation ceremony; as each graduate crosses the stage, he or she shakes hands not only with his high school principal but also with his middle and elementary school principals. The principals in this particular team said that the first meeting held with all of the entities to get the "project" off the ground was one of the most powerful events in their lives.

English language art teachers are in the best position to serve as catalysts for other disciplines; after all, their main goal is to ensure the success of written and oral communications. Therefore, they are naturals!

The Role of the Middle School in Vertical Articulation

I theorize that the most advantageous place and perhaps the most appropriate place to start visualizing vertical connectedness is from the *middle*. At the top of the hill, looking back at the students' progress to this point and moving them, challenging them, and encouraging them, all the while envisioning/imagining their successful graduation from high school and a satisfying life after that.

Middle level teachers have many qualities that make this the best place to begin vertical articulation: 1) they are child centered; 2) they are willing to explore and experiment; 3) they are nurturing and compassionate; 4) they are willing to take risks; and 5) they are cooperative and collaborative. Although teachers at the other levels may have all or some of these qualities, the middle level teacher should have these qualities in a more highly developed form. These are almost a necessity for teachers who work with adolescents, who experience more change between grades 6 and 8 than at any other time in life except early infancy.

So teachers in middle level schools are in the best position to help vertical seamlessness come to be in our school districts. Convene some sessions at your area affiliate meetings and middle school conferences. Together we can make "vertical connectedness" a schoolwide expression. It's a necessary piece in the middle school mosaic.

References

Lounsbury, J. and H. Johnston. (1985). *The ninth grader: A profile.* In T. F. Koerner (Ed.), *How fares the ninth grade?: A day in the life of a ninth grader.* Reston, VA: National Association of Secondary School Principals.

NCTE's Position on the teaching of English: Assumptions and practices. (1991). Urbana, IL: National Council of Teachers of English.

Wells, M. Cyrene. (1996). *Literacies Lost: When students move from a progressive middle school to a traditional high school.* New York: Teachers College Press.

Lanny van Allen is a past chair of NCTE's Junior High/Middle School Assembly and, from its inception, has served as professional publications editor for *Voices from the Middle*. Van Allen serves as a consultant for the University of Texas Reading and Language Arts Center and for the Holt, Rinehart, and Winston textbook publishers. She was a classroom teacher in English language arts for fifteen years and then worked in English language arts curriculum at the Texas Education Agency. Van Allen has presented many articles and conference sessions on vertical connectedness, among other topics.

Appendix 1
The Middle School Mosaic:
A Brief History

The Middle School Mosaic grew out of NCTE middle level educators' need to have a stronger voice and greater visibility in the Council and to have an opportunity at the annual convention and spring conference to network with other middle level educators. In 1996, at the Secondary Section Committee's July retreat in Indianapolis, Indiana, we identified twelve issues requiring action, including the middle level educators' needs. Key leaders in the middle level community were invited to meet with Secondary Section Committee members, Executive Committee members, and NCTE staff at a brainstorming breakfast on Friday, November 22, during the 1996 Annual Convention in Chicago. Groups represented at this initial session were the Secondary and Elementary Section Committees, Junior High/Middle School Assembly, *Voices from the Middle*, the *English Journal*, ALAN, CEE Commission on Middle Grades English Language Arts Teacher Education, and CEL Commission on Middle/Junior High Schools. Having a block of time at the annual convention to feature specially coordinated sessions and activities for middle level educators including those involved in teacher education was one of the short-term solutions proposed.

In 1997 at the January convention planning meeting at NCTE Headquarters, Elizabeth Close, Middle School Representative to the Secondary Section Committee; Katherine Ramsey, Secondary Section Committee member; Brenda Hollon-Craig, chair of the Junior High/Middle School Assembly; Karen Smith, associate executive director; and Leslie Froeschl, administrative assistant to Karen Smith, met to plan the first middle school colloquium within the Annual Convention program at Detroit, Michigan, held in the fall of 1997. The title of Martha Magner's joint program proposal from the Junior High/Middle School Assembly and the CEE Commission on Middle Grades English Language Arts Teacher Education, "A Middle School Mosaic: Putting Together the Pieces," summarized the previous discussion among all of the groups so well that the planning group adopted the title as the theme of the colloquium. To differentiate it from the whole-day concept of the Conference on Whole Language, the planners saw the designated period as twenty-four plus hours beginning with a double session on Friday afternoon, November 21, 1998, and ending with a reception late Saturday afternoon, November 22. The program was entitled "A Middle School Mosaic: What a Difference a Day Makes."

The resulting program featured sessions chosen by middle level convention proposal readers: Elizabeth Close and Katherine Ramsey from the Secondary Section Committee; Yvonne Siu-Runyan and Donna Maxim from the Elementary Section Committee; Alfredo Lujan and Debbie Allen from the

Rainbow Strand planners, and Brenda Hollon-Craig from the Junior High/ Middle School Assembly. The middle level planners especially appreciated the encouragement and support of Council leaders Carol Avery, Sheridan Blau, and Joan Naomi Steiner and associate executive directors Karen Smith and Charlie Suhor.

The keynote session, "A Middle School Mosaic: Putting the Pieces Together," was planned for Friday afternoon from 12:45–3:45 p.m. Four concurrent sessions were slated from 8:30–9:45 a.m. on Saturday morning. Other concurrent sessions were planned for Saturday afternoon from 12:15–1:30 p.m. (5), 2:00–3:15 p.m. (4), and 3:45–5:00 p.m. (4).

To conclude the special middle level event, reading specialist Kylene Beers invited key middle level educators to present an interactive mini workshop about reading at the middle level from 2:00–5:00 p.m. Other middle school sessions were scattered throughout the convention, but the planners hoped that the twenty-four-hour concentrated format would be especially appealing to local educators or those who had a limited amount of leave from their schools for the NCTE Annual Convention.

In addition to the specifically identified sessions, the Middle School Mosaic planners proposed several special events to build community among middle level educators. The first special event, from 9:45–11:00 a.m on Saturday, was "Coffee with the Middle School," a time for middle level educators to meet with leaders from the various interest groups, middle level publications, and NCTE middle level authors. Between 11:30 and 1:00 p.m. middle levelers could choose between the Elementary Books for Children Luncheon and the Secondary Section Luncheon or have lunch on their own. The Middle School Mosaic ended with a reception sponsored by Christopher-Gordon Publishers, Simon and Schuster, Scholastic, and Bantam Doubleday Dell and a business meeting for the Junior High/Middle School Assembly at which the second recipient of the Assembly's Richard W. Halle Award for an outstanding contributor to middle level education, Lanny van Allen, was announced.

To give cohesiveness to the Mosaic the planners requested that the keynote session, mini-workshop, reception, and business meeting all occur at the same location. Local area educator Toby Curry agreed to gather middle school art from the Dewey Center for Urban Education to decorate the middle level area. To publicize the event, headquarters sent special advance flyers to all middle level educators on the NCTE roster. Special invitations were extended to council leaders for the reception and to local middle level teachers for the Middle School Mosaic. Elizabeth Close and Katherine Ramsey prepared an article about the Middle School Mosaic for the *Council Chronicle*. As an additional enticement for middle level educators, a separate program for the Middle School Mosaic was available. Finally, the convention program featured information about the Middle School Mosaic and highlighted the Mosaic and other sessions of interest to middle level educators.

The first Middle School Mosaic did provide a much-needed forum for middle level educators within the existing structure of the Council and a promising beginning for a stronger presence in the middle. At the planning session in Urbana for the 1998 Annual Convention in Nashville, Tennessee, the Secondary Section Committee recommended that the Mosaic be continued.

Plans were made to continue the middle level colloquium with a format similar to that of 1997. Carolyn Lott, chair of the section, suggested a book be developed.

At the 1998 Spring Conference in Albuquerque, New Mexico, Peter Feely, an acquisitions editor at NCTE, met with Elizabeth Close and Katherine Ramsey to propose a brief publication to celebrate the Middle School Mosaic concept and to capture its essence for middle level educators who did not attend the convention in Detroit. The participants from the first Mosaic were invited to submit written versions of their sessions.

These vignettes are a representative sampling of the diverse and rewarding sessions of NCTE's first special event specifically for middle level educators. We hope that these pieces preserve some of the excitement that the planners and presenters felt about this auspicious beginning.

Appendix 2
A Middle School Mosaic:
What a Difference a Day Makes

FRIDAY
12:45–3:45 p.m.

MIDDLE SCHOOL MOSAIC: PUTTING TOGETHER THE PIECES
Mini-Workshop/Roundtable Discussion sponsored by the Junior High/Middle School Assembly and the CEE Commission for Middle School Teacher Education.
Cobo Center/Meeting Room D3–28 (Detroit "Gold" Zone, 3rd Level, Room 28)

Speaker: Michael R. Strickland, Jersey City State College, New Jersey, "Exploring our Multicultural World through Poetry"

Table Number	Presenter and Topic
1	Ross M. Burkhardt, Shoreham-Wading River Middle School, Shoreham, New York, "Writing Across the Curriculum in Middle School"
2	Rita S. Brause, Fordham University, New York, New York, "Reflection on an Urban Middle School Writers Workshop"
3	Lois T. Stover, St. Mary's College of Maryland, St. Mary's City, "Interdisciplinary Teaming in the Middle School"
4	Lanny van Allen, Texas Education Agency, Austin, "Vertical Teaming—Including the Middle School"
5	Judith Hayn, Auburn University, Alabama, and Beverly Corley, Sanford Middle School, Opelika, Alabama, "Portfolios in an Integrated Setting in Middle School"
6	Martha Magner, A. MacArthur Barr Middle School, Nanuet, New York, "Why Middle School Advisory? Why Middle School Service Learning"
7	Katherine D. Ramsey, West Ridge Middle School, Austin, Texas, "Literature Circles in the Middle School: Learning to Talk about Books"
8	Richard W. Halle, Marshfield Junior High School, Wisconsin, "Who Is the Middle School Student"
9	Lisa A. Spiegel, University of South Dakota, Vermillion, "Young Adult Authors: The Problem Novel"
10	Brenda Hollon-Craig, The Archer School for Girls, Pacific Palisades, California, "Who's Afraid of the Big Bad Web? Computers Can Be Tamed"

SATURDAY
8:30–9:45 a.m.

E Sessions

THE ART OF COMPASSIONATE IMAGINING IN HISTORICAL NARRATIVES OF CHILDREN AT WORK
Examines the issue of children at work in different types of settings within fiction and nonfiction narratives, and the manner in which authors create reader empathy for the child protagonist.
Cobo Center/Meeting Room D3–26 and 27 (Detroit "Gold" Zone, 3rd Level, Rooms 26 and 27)

Speakers: Karen Patricia Smith, Queens College Graduate School of Library and Information Studies, Flushing, New York, "'Love's Labour Won': The Imagery of Empathy in Ann Rinaldi's *The Blue Door*"; Marcia Baghban, Queens College, CUNY, New York, "Working in and between Two Cultures: Moonshadow's Dilemma in Laurence Yep's *Dragonwings*"; Myra Zarnowski, Queens College, CUNY, New York, "Telling Lewis Hine's Story: Russell Freedman's *Kids at Work*"

SO YOU WANT TO BE A STORYTELLER: STORYTELLING, THE INTERACTIVE LANGUAGE EXPERIENCE
Includes hands-on experience to discover the hows and whys of storytelling in the classroom.
Cobo Center/Meeting Room D3–16, 17, and 18 (Detroit "Gold" Zone, 3rd Level, Rooms 16, 17, and 18)

Speakers: Glenda Harris, Liberty Bell Middle School, Johnson City, Tennessee; Suzie Booker, Iowa City, Iowa

INTEGRATED STUDIES IN THE MIDDLE SCHOOL CLASSROOM
Ways students raised questions and investigated social injustice through novels and community inquiry and action; strategies for linking the prose of fiction with which students are familiar to the discourse of science in ways that improve comprehension of science books, grades 4–12; and the basis for a study of the history and laws of U.S. immigration by learning the stories of first generation immigrants through interviews.
Cobo Center/ Meeting Room D3–25 (Detroit "Gold" Zone, 3rd Level, Room 25)

Speakers: Beverly Busching, University of South Carolina, Columbia, and Betty Ann Slesinger, Campus R—IMO, Columbia, South Carolina, "Third Class Is More Than a Cruise Ship Ticket: Seventh Graders Look at Social Forces"; Petey Young, Southern Oregon University, Ashland, "Footprints in the Mud"; Michael Gerard, Mary Institute and St. Louis Country Day School, Missouri, "Fostering Empathy: An Integrated Study of Immigrants' Stories"

HOMELAND: MORAL ACTIONS THROUGH ORAL HISTORIES
Emphasizes oral histories that have long been passed down for entertaining and teaching morals as the embodiment of trust, faith, compassion, and good will among storytellers and listeners.

Cobo Center/Meeting Room D3–24 (Detroit "Gold" Zone, 3rd Level, Room 24)

Speakers: Alfredo Celedon Lujan, Pojoaque Valley Schools, Santa Fe, New Mexico, "So S-Weate and Other *Historias*"; Vicki Hunt, Peoria High School, Arizona, "Homeland: Tracing Roots through Oral Histories"

DISRUPTING DEMON"ISMS": CREATIVE ARTS AND LITERATURE IN THE MORAL DOMAIN
Presents strategies for using literature and the arts to explore moral dilemmas.
Cobo Center/Meeting Room D3–20 (Detroit "Gold" Zone, 3rd Level, Room 20)

Speakers: Marlene Ann Birkman, Webster University, St. Louis, Missouri, "Poetry in Public Places"; Cheryl Silberberg Grossman, University of Missouri, Kansas City, "Cotton Club Time: The Harlem Renaissance through Poetry and Music"; Janet E. Kaufman, University of Utah, Salt Lake City, "Scripting Our Lives with Cormier's *Tunes for Bears to Dance to*: From Powerlessness and Helplessness to Strength and Forgiveness"; Mary M. Krogness, Hathaway Brown School, Shaker Heights, Ohio, "Getting to the Heart of Literature through Classroom Drama"

9:45–11:00 a.m.

COFFEE WITH THE MIDDLE SCHOOL
Anyone interested in junior high/middle school education is invited to attend this mid-morning social hour to meet and talk informally with people actively working on middle school issues through their groups, committees, or publications.
Cobo Center/Meeting Room D3–28 (Detroit "Gold" Zone, 3rd Level, Room 28)

Table Number	Participating Group/Author
1	NCTE Membership Table, including representatives from the Elementary Section Steering Committee, Secondary Section Steering Committee, and the Middle Level Representative-at-Large.
2	*English Journal* Editor
3	*Language Arts* Editors
4	*Voices from the Middle* Editors
5	ALAN (Assembly on Literature for Adolescents of NCTE)
6	CEE Commission on Middle Grades English Language Arts
7	Junior High/Middle School Assembly
8	National Middle School Association
9	Kylene Beers (NCTE Author)
10	Scott R. Christian (NCTE Author)
11	Margaret J. Finders (NCTE Author)
12	Teri S. Lesesne (NCTE Author)

11:30 a.m.–1:30 p.m.

SECTION LUNCHEONS

ELEMENTARY BOOKS FOR CHILDREN LUNCHEON
Westin/Columbus Room, Level 4

Speaker: Walter Dean Myers, author of *Harlem, How Mr. Monkey Saw the Whole World, Shadow of the Red Moon, Fallen Angels*, and *Scorpions*

SECONDARY SECTION LUNCHEON
Westin/Cartier Room, Level 4

Speaker: Julia Alvarez, Middlebury College, Vermont, author of *How the García Girls Lost Their Accents, In the Time of Butterflies*, and *Yo!*

12:15–1:30 p.m.

F Sessions

COMING FACE-TO-FACE WITH THE TRADITIONS AND VALUES OF CULTURALLY DIVERSE PEOPLE BY EXPLORING THEIR FOLKTALES
Presents ways folktales, myths, and legends can help students value the traditions, beliefs, and attitudes of their own and other cultures, and engage in dialogue about important social issues.
Cobo Center/Meeting Room M3–31 (Macomb "Orange" Zone, 3rd Level, Room 31)

Speakers: Lucia Gonzales, Scholastic, Inc., New York, New York; Laura Robb, Powhatan School, Boyce, Virginia, and Scholastic, Inc., New York, New York, "Exploring Unprompted Reactions to Folktales in Writing Workshop"; Baba Wagué Diakité, Scholastic Press, New York, New York, "We Must Teach Our Children"

THE POWER OF COMPOSING LITERACY NARRATIVES: FOR TEACHER-AUTHORS, FOR STUDENTS, FOR PARENTS
Discusses teachers' writing of literacy narratives about their own students and shows the powerful impact that writing has had on themselves, on those students, and on the parents of those students.
Cobo Center/Meeting Room D3–26 and 27 (Detroit "Gold" Zone, 3rd level, Rooms 26 and 27)

Speakers: Cathy Fleischer, Eastern Michigan University, Ypsilanti, "The Impact on Teacher-Authors"; Julie King, Holmes Middle School, Livonia, Michigan, "The Impact on Students"; Jennifer Hannick, Ann Arbor, Michigan, "The Impact on Parents"

THE WRITER'S NOTEBOOK: A PLACE TO THINK
Ways to use the writer's notebook as a place to refine and extend thinking.
Cobo Center/Meeting Room D3–25 (Detroit "Gold" Zone, 3rd Level, Room 25)

Speakers: Janet Angelillo, Teachers College, Columbia University, New York, New York; Anna Danon Reduce, Teachers College, Columbia University, New York, New York

HONORING DIVERSITY: TRANSITIONS IN CONTENT AREA CURRIC-
ULA, LANGUAGE ARTS INSTRUCTION, AND ASSESSMENT
In recognition of the increasingly diverse student population found in classrooms today, various changes in content area curricula, instructional strategies, and alternative assessment measures are presented.
Cobo Center/Meeting Room D3–16, 17, and 18 (Detroit "Gold" Zone, 3rd Level, Rooms 16, 17, and 18)

Presenter: Elaine M. Bukowiecki, Lesley College, Cambridge, Massachusetts

2:00–3:15 p.m.

G Sessions

JULIE OF THE WOLVES: A SILVER ANNIVERSARY CELEBRATION
Response to this classic novel by the author, a teacher of Native children, and a critic.
Cobo Center/Meeting Room D3–16, 17, and 18 (Detroit "Gold" Zone, 3rd Level, Rooms 16, 17, and 18)

Speakers: Jean Craighead George, author, HarperCollins Publishers, New York, New York, "Creating Julie"; Rosemary Doyle, Q.S.I. International School, Ljubljana, Slovenia, "Julie Speaks to Us: Native Children Respond"; Jon C. Stott, University of Alberta, Edmonton, Canada, "The Many Faces of Julie: A Critic's Response"

READING IS STUPID: WORKING WITH RELUCTANT OR RESISTANT
READERS
Explores the literacy experiences of reluctant readers and ways to let them in to the secrets of what engaged readers know and do.
Cobo Center/Meeting Room D3–19 (Detroit "Gold" Zone, 3rd Level, Room 19)

Presenter: Jeff Wilhelm, University of Maine, Orono

ACKNOWLEDGING LONGINGS: POETRY FOR AND WITH TEENAGERS
An exploration of the longings and yearnings that prevail during adolescence and give us a basis for expression.
Cobo Center/Meeting Room D3–20 (Detroit "Gold" Zone, 3rd Level, Room 20)

Presenter: Kathi Appelt, College Station, Texas

IDENTITIES, MEMOIRS, AND AMERICAN DREAMS: A CROSS-AGE WRIT-
ING AND LITERATURE EXCHANGE USING ELECTRONIC MAIL
*Explores the interesting concept of cross-age partnerships and the successful
integration of online computer technology.*
Cobo Center/Meeting Room D3–22 (Detroit "Gold" Zone, 3rd Level, Room 22)

Speakers: Heather J. Borden, Kosciusko Junior High School, Mississippi, "The
Identity Box"; Sharon McKenna Ladner, Pascagoula High School, Mississippi,
"Memoirs"; Roseanne Baca Lara, Gadsden Middle School, Anthony, New
Mexico, "American Dreams"

2:00–5:00 p.m.

GH Session

MIDDLE SCHOOL READERS: MAKING THEM AND KEEPING THEM
*Mini-workshop highlighting ways to connect middle schoolers with reading in their
literature and content area classes.*
Cobo Center/Meeting Room D3–28 (Detroit "Gold" Zone, 3rd Level, Room 28)

Presenters: Richard F. Abrahamson, University of Houston, Texas, "Middle
Schoolers and Reading: How the Twain Shall Meet"; Kylene Beers, Sam
Houston State University, Houston, Texas, "Why Some Middle Schoolers Just
Say No—To Reading"; Robert E. Probst, Georgia State University, Atlanta,
"Eliciting Response from Middle Schoolers: Or, Extracting Matter from Black
Holes"; Linda Rief, Oyster River Middle School and University of New
Hampshire, Durham, "Reading Choices: Reading Voices"

Table Number	Discussion Leader and Topic
1	Judy M. Wallis, Alief Independent School District, Houston, Texas, "Comprehension Strategies for When They Just Don't Get It"
2	Donald R. Gallo, Central Connecticut State University, New Britain (Retired), "Getting There Shortly: Short Stories that Entice Readers"
3	Liz C. Stephens, Southwest Texas State University, San Marcos, "Internet and Interest: Using Technology to Create Readers"
4	Mary Santerre, The Village School, Houston, Texas, "Thematic Units in the Middle School"
5	Hollis Lowery-Moore, Sam Houston State University, Huntsville, Texas, "Understanding Why Middle Schoolers Don't Read"
6	Marilyn Melton and Karen Oliphant, River Oaks Baptist School, Houston, Texas, "When Reading Leads to Writing: How to Turn Response into Themes"
7	Margaret Hill, University of Houston, Clear Lake, Texas, "When They Can't Read: How to Help Middle Schoolers Learn to Decode"

3:45–5:00 p.m.

H Sessions

WORDS OF WITNESS, VOICES OF HOPE: LITERATURE AND LESSONS OF THE HOLOCAUST FOR MIDDLE SCHOOL
An adaptable English-Social Studies unit addressing prejudice and individual responsibility and fostering empathy for human experience.
Cobo Center/Meeting Room M3–31 (Macomb "Orange" Zone, 3rd Level, Room 31)

Speakers: Karen Zelde Schejtman Sultan, Takoma Park Middle School, Silver Spring, Maryland, "Mini-Units to Find and Construct Meaning from the Holocaust"; Marlene Hartstein, Takoma Park Middle School, Silver Spring, Maryland, "Genre of the Holocaust for Middle School Students"; Leila Christenbury, Richmond, Virginia, "Eloquence at Eleven—The Voices of Students"

WILL HOBBS: AN AUTHOR FOR INQUIRING YOUNG MINDS
Using the young adult novels of Will Hobbs to lead to exploration of a wide variety of topics and the reading of diverse literature.
Cobo Center/Meeting Room D3–16, 17, and 18 (Detroit "Gold" Zone, 3rd Level, Rooms 16, 17, and 18)

Speakers: Will Hobbs, author, Morrow Junior Books, New York, New York, "Bearstone and Beyond: Exploring and Learning in the Natural World"; Elizabeth Poe, Radford University, Virginia, "Ever-Expanding Literature Circles Inspired by the Novels of Will Hobbs: An Interdisciplinary Author Study and Much, Much More!"

THE REVOLUTION CONTINUES
Some extraordinary middle school success stories in inner-city Detroit brought about by multiple years in two powerful whole language classrooms.
Cobo Center/Meeting Room D3–20 (Detroit "Gold" Zone, 3rd Level, Room 20)

Speakers: Toby Kahn Curry, Dewey Center for Urban Education, Detroit, Michigan; Kevin La Plante, Dewey Center for Urban Education, Detroit, Michigan

5:15–6:15 p.m.

MIDDLE SCHOOL MOSAIC SOCIAL HOUR
Junior high/middle school educators are invited to celebrate the first year of special middle school activities at a social hour.
Cobo Center/Meeting Room D3–28 (Detroit "Gold" Zone, 3rd Level, Room 28)

Sponsored by Christopher-Gordon Publishers, Simon and Schuster, Scholastic, and Bantam Doubleday Dell.

6:30–7:30 p.m.

JUNIOR HIGH/MIDDLE SCHOOL ASSEMBLY BUSINESS MEETING
Cobo Center/Meeting Room D3–25 (Detroit "Gold" Zone, 3rd Level, Room 25)

Editors

Elizabeth Close taught middle level grades for thirty-two years, twenty-eight of them at Farnsworth Middle School in Guilderland, New York. She is currently director of Educational Outreach for the National Research Center on English Learning and Achievement (CELA) at the University at Albany, State University of New York. A milestone in her career occurred in 1988 when she first became affiliated with the Center for Learning and Teaching, directed by Arthur Applebee, Judith Langer, and Alan Purvis. That center grew into CELA. This experience gave Close and her students unique opportunities to reflect and grow as thinkers and learners.

Close has been active in NCTE, serving as associate chair of the Secondary Section Steering Committee and on the Executive Committee. She has worked for the New York State Education Department as a consultant and has presented many workshops and conferences. She was named the Edwin A. Hoey winner by NCTE in 1999, received a Paul and Kate Farmer Award in 1993 for an article in *English Journal*, and has been recognized at the district and state levels for her teaching achievements. She is co-editor of "Middle Talk," a column in *English Journal* and is a member of the CEE Commission on Middle Level English Language Arts Teaching.

Katherine D. Ramsey teaches sixth-grade English language arts at River Oaks Baptist School. She has taught at the middle level for eighteen years in both public and private schools in Texas and Massachusetts. Ramsey credits her college professor mother with instilling in her a passion for life-long learning and a love of teaching. Her special interest is creating a literate environment in a student-centered classroom where middle level students can explore their own potential through language. Learning with and from her inquisitive, diverse pupils has been as exciting and surprising as the young people themselves. Ramsey is a long-time member of NCTE. She currently serves on the Executive Committee, as the associate chair of the Secondary Section Steering Committee, and coeditor of "Middle Talk," the middle level column in the *English Journal*. She has been chair of the Junior High/Middle School Assembly and Secondary Section Nominating Committee and a member of the CEE Commission on Middle Level English Language Arts Teacher Preparation. A frequent presenter at local and national conferences, Ramsey received the Richard W. Halle Outstanding Middle Level Educator Award in 1998 from the Junior High/ Middle School Assembly.

This book was set in Palatino and Helvetica by Electronic Imaging.
Typefaces used on the cover and spine are Elli, by the Font Bureau,
and Mason Sans, by Emigre.
The book was printed on 50-lb. Husky Offset by IPC Communication Services.